On Happiness

On Happiness

On Happiness

New Ideas for the Twenty-First Century

Edited by Camilla Nelson,
Deborah Pike & Georgina Ledvinka

UWA PUBLISHING

First published in 2015
by UWA Publishing
Crawley, Western Australia 6009
www.uwap.uwa.edu.au

UWAP is an imprint of UWA Publishing,
a division of The University of Western Australia

THE UNIVERSITY OF
WESTERN AUSTRALIA

National Library of Australia
Cataloguing-in-Publication entry

On happiness: new ideas for the twenty-first century/ edited by Camilla Nelson, Deborah Pike and Georgina Ledvinka

9781742586076 (paperback)
Includes bibliographical references.

Social prediction—Australia.
Happiness—Australia.
Happiness—Philosophy.
Australia—Social conditions—21st century.
Australia—Forecasting.

303.4994

 This project has been assisted by the Australian Government through the Australia Council, its arts funding and advisory body.

Cover image: Rene Magritte *Hegels Holiday* 1958 © Rene Magritte/ADAGP. Licensed by Viscopy, 2015

Typeset by J & M Typesetting

Printed by Griffin Press

CONTENTS

ACKNOWLEDGEMENTS

The editors would like to express their deep gratitude to Terri-ann White for taking on this project at UWA Publishing and Katie Connolly for her editorial support. The idea for this essay collection arose from our research seminar series at UNDA and a subsequent symposium that was generously supported by the research office at UNDA. Thank you also to John Rees for his sagacious advice and assistance throughout. This is a peer-reviewed publication, and we would also like to thank the many anonymous referees for their valuable comments. Last but never least, we would like to thank all of our contributors for their time, intelligence and dedication.

Camilla Nelson, Deborah Pike and Georgina Ledvinka

THIS BOOK WON'T MAKE YOU HAPPY

Camilla Nelson and Deborah Pike

Happiness is often said to be a transparent emotion: you know it when you feel it. But if you think a little further about the problems it evokes – in politics, philosophy and economics – happiness turns out to be something of a paradox. Indeed, happiness has been characterised as both an illusion and delusion; a shimmering dream; but also as a physical state that can be medically verified using a range of neurological indicators. It is an ideal that encapsulates everything that is worthy and desirable, but is also a lucrative commodity to be bought and sold, earning millions of dollars for motivational gurus on the self-help circuit. In Western societies, happiness has come to be regarded as something of a right; it has been enshrined in legal and political documents. And while it is commonly presented as an object of universal striving, it is equally an idea with a history that can be located within a specific time and place, with distinct cultural and temporal variations.

This essay collection traces the contours of this paradoxical ideal, and the strategies that have been – and are constantly being – devised to acquire it. It brings together perspectives on happiness from diverse fields of inquiry, including ethics, philosophy, economics, psychology, sociology and the arts in order to encourage readers to reflect critically on what the pursuit of happiness might actually mean. In this sense, the collection is something of a provocation. Each essay has been designed to interrogate a 'common sense' understanding of happiness, in order to provoke us into shaking off our capacity for self-absorption, and inspire us to instead take action against the problems that confront us as a society, whether these are war and conflict, climate change, poverty, or the means to maintain an educational system that fosters active and thinking citizens. While offering some positive ways forward for creating a happier life, this book has not been designed to 'make you happy' so much as to suggest that there is a need to reconstitute not only the happiness of society, but also the idea of happiness itself.

Indeed, it is difficult to think seriously about happiness without first acknowledging that there is a multi-billion dollar industry out there awash with books, guides and all sorts of experts promising that certain kinds of happiness are yours for the making or taking in a matter of days, or even hours. 'Choose to Be Happy', runs the type on the back of the archetypal self-help book. 'Choose to Rise Above Anxiety, Anger, and Depression'. 'Find More Hope, Love and Confidence' and 'Be the Person You Really Want to Be'. With so much happiness for sale, it would seem that the current corporate pitch on happiness is demanding nothing less than shiny perfection. But is happiness really just a matter of personal attitude, of changing the way that you look at the world? Might false optimism actually lead to failure rather than success?

Clive Hamilton asks exactly this question in 'The Lies of Happiness', the opening essay of this book, in which he distinguishes between happiness based on an authentic and socially located sense of self, and the sorts of benign fictions and self-deceptions in which most of us indulge in order to bolster our self-confidence and avoid worry and pain. Hamilton suggests that these trivial fictions are not as harmless as they might first appear because they leave us open to exploitation by those he calls the 'clever manipulators' and 'makers of brands' of the wider 'money culture'. Rather than encouraging people to take control of their lives, Hamilton argues that these illusions are more likely to foster a kind of insecure narcissism that discourages any examination of the social circumstances in which we live. Happiness based on an inauthentic sense of self, divorced from material reality and circumstance, gives us not freedom, but a dangerous illusion of independence.

One of the central features of the happiness industry seems to be that it places all the emphasis on you – your attitudes, your feelings, your aspirations. If happiness were a branding strategy it would be one that was based on identity and independence, with a tight focus on lifestyle, passion, imagination and personal power. A whole swathe of astonishingly successful advertising campaigns immediately spring to mind, including advertisements for iPhones, iPods and iPads, not to mention the decades long Nike campaign that trumpets the idea that achievement and goal-building is all about self belief: 'Just do it', says Nike. Don't think. Be happy. According to seasoned misanthropist Barbara Ehrenreich, the lack of reality engendered by an unwarranted emphasis on positive feelings, such as that which she associates with the 'father' of positive psychology, Martin Seligman, has contributed to cyclical stock market carnage, and is – in intellectual terms – only one small step away from the idea that happy thoughts can cure cancer.[1]

The idea that happiness is purely a matter of personal attitude may encourage some people to take control of their lives or to consider they are capable of change. But there is a problem in the way that the idea engenders a wider political dynamic that invites us to blame social problems on the individual. If you believe the self-esteem mantras – the idea that positive things comes to those who believe in themselves strongly enough – then it seems that you are required to believe that everything comes back not to material situations, but to personal character. The failure to be happy, to attain certain goals, is blamed on deficiencies of self-worth, self-motivation or self-belief, when in reality the barriers to human flourishing are just as likely – if not more likely – to be functional, material and economic. There is often no lack of aspirational goals in people's lives – to be smart, get a good job, go to university – but there are very often barriers to realisation. There is a pressing need therefore not to be blinded by superficial questions of attitude, but to start with material situations. Indeed, part of the problem is that to always see the glass as half full actually requires you to disregard the empty half – that is, to disregard the facts.

Economists have historically been great collectors of facts. But, as John Quiggin points out in his essay 'What Happiness Conceals', the facts of human happiness are often elusive. This has not stopped happiness research from becoming a booming field in economics, growing steadily since the 1970s when Jigme Singye Wangchuck announced at his coronation as king of Bhutan that his reign would be one that focused on Gross National Happiness rather than Gross National Product. Since then, mighty careers have been launched through the creation of a range of economic instruments to measure happiness, and prizes bestowed. But, according to Quiggin, the most significant finding to emerge from certain sections of this burgeoning field is the discovery that happiness is relative and subjective. Even this finding may be an illusion, argues Quiggin, and the world's economists would perhaps get a lot further if they stopped asking about the emotional sources of happiness, and started thinking about the causes of human misery. These include poverty, conflict, hunger and disease, phenomena which are numerous, measurable, objective and real. Focusing on material interventions such as poverty alleviation may sound significantly less glamorous for economists than a focus on inner feeling and emotion, but much of the world's population would be significantly better off. The theme of happy economics returns later in the volume, with J. K. Gibson-Graham, Jenny Cameron and Stephen Healy's chapter on new 'relational' economic measures of happiness, and David Ritter similarly stressing the modern capabilities approach pioneered by Amartya Sen, which focuses on human 'welfare' rather than emotional happiness, defined through a list of objective capabilities.[2]

Meanwhile, in affluent nations the culture of conspicuous consumption grows apace. Whether it is a McDonald's 'Happy Meal', or the gratification afforded by the purchase of a strawberry daiquiri made with melted water from a 3,000-year-old iceberg, we are living in a culture that relentlessly endorses the idea that people are made happier with every acquisition. Scrolling through Tweets, Facebook updates and Instagram photos, an innocent onlooker could be forgiven for thinking that they are missing out on all the fun – that their life is not as happy, exciting and fulfilled as the next person's. In this respect the subjective and relative nature of happiness presents something of a problem. In the digital age, people often present online versions of themselves which are luminous, ecstatic, and surrounded by friends – replete with photographs of holidays in brilliant tropical light, boyfriends, babies – leaving the rest of us feeling bound by unmet desires and frustrations. In his essay 'Loving Happiness but Feeling Sad' Brock Bastian investigates the unexpected psychological effects of the Western cultural obsession with happiness, arguing that an increasing social pressure to be happy may actually have detrimental consequences for an individual's emotional functioning. Bastian's essay highlights the deleterious effects when normal levels of sadness, grief or anxiety are routinely pathologised so that even superficial despondency is treated through an array of drugs or therapeutic interventions designed to bring the individual back to 'health'. Bastian argues that pain and sadness are important human experiences, and can have positive outcomes. Painful emotions tell us significant things about the ways in which we are interacting with our environment and other people, and whether those interactions are successful. Ironically, Bastian also points out that the cultural emphasis on happy or so-called healthy emotions also result in people evaluating themselves more negatively when they do feel sad, generating a greater intensity of negative emotion in their daily lives. Ultimately, the cultural pressure to be happy may actually be the very thing that is making us sad.

This is one of the many reasons why Martha Nussbaum, one of the most prescient critics of the happiness movement of the present day, has argued that other emotions are also, if not more, important – anger can give rise to action, cynicism can give rise to the kind of critical mindset through which leaps and bounds in knowledge are made, and though misery may be unattractive, it has also given rise to astonishing works of art. Empathy, community and social bonding more commonly arise from an experience of sadness, a capacity to sense the pain and misfortune others.[3] In short, unless the full range of human emotions are considered we risk becoming lost in our atomised worlds of allegedly happy self-perfection. Our happy sparkling selves might even be said to impose a kind of social conformity, a set of cultural constrictions within which we are destined to jump around like the figures in *The Lego Movie*, blindly following 'The Instructions' and endlessly chanting 'Everything is Awesome'.

Happiness of this sort is one of the many illusions that Kurt Vonnegut acerbically sweeps away in his essay collection, *A Man Without a Country*. In lines resurrected from *Cat's Cradle*, Vonnegut locates happiness as a form of self-deception, as a way of hiding from the world's uncomfortable realities. He writes,

> I wanted all things to seem to make some sense,
> So we could all be happy, yes, instead of tense.
> And I made up lies, so
> they all fit nice,
> and I made this sad world
> a paradise.[4]

Happiness of this delusional if not downright sinister sort is famously the subject of Aldous Huxley's dystopian novel *Brave New World*, in which Huxley envisaged a political regime that clings onto power by instilling a form of chemically induced happiness – called soma – into the rest of society. In a world in which sales of new generation antidepressants such as

Prozac and Zoloft are surging higher, it may even be that Huxley's dystopian political scenario is becoming increasingly – not less – relevant.

Far from being a noncomplex good, on closer scrutiny, happiness turns out to be ethically fraught. The morally complex nature of happiness is perhaps best illustrated in the politically charged usages to which happiness research is commonly put. Happiness is beloved of the left, who understand it as an instrument to guide debate beyond the narrow confines of the economy. Happiness is beloved of conservatives who see it as a means of preserving the status quo. Happiness is beloved of environmentalists who see it as a means of constituting an alternative form of ethics that may give rise to a sustainable future. Even big business likes happiness because happy people are more productive workers.

Further anomalies are thrown up by the findings of social scientific research on happiness, which often sit well with entrenched social norms, or else foreground a social reality from which ideology never seems to be far away. It is perhaps unsurprising that having a job will make you happy, for example. But oddly enough, according to the Easterlin Paradox, the money gained from work apparently won't.[5] Hence, if income is unrelated to happiness, why spend billions on a welfare safety net? Why bother with minimum wages? Indeed, one of the most persistent, if controversial, findings of the social scientific research on happiness is that if you want to be happy then you should never ever have children.[6] Being married will apparently make you happy, but having children will only bring you anxiety, aggravation and grief. But is this the kind of world in which we really want to live?

In 'Anger and Courage: the Daughters of Hope', philosopher Richard Hamilton cuts to the heart of the ethical dilemmas associated with happiness studies, critiquing the popular idea that a positive mental attitude can change reality, a view which he argues is predicated on the false assumption that the world is 'just' and that benefits and harm are distributed according to merit. Hamilton traces some of these views back to the understanding of mental attitude associated with the Greek Stoics, who argued that the proper mental state is one which recognises the distinction between matters that fall within our own powers and those which do not. He argues that there are also dangers in this view, as it often results in political quietism in the face of great injustice and neglects the fact that human beings can, with sufficient determination, change the world rather than simply accept it as is. Anger and courage, according to St Augustine of Hippo, are the daughters of hope, and both may be required to make the world a happier place, but there is a need to distinguish between false hope and the sort of hope that is necessary to change the world for the better.

It is not only happiness that is difficult. It turns out that we have a problem with pleasure, too. In his essay, 'Blissed Out – on Hedonophobia', Steven Connor explores the roots of the Western idea of happiness in the 'Felicific Calculus' of Jeremy Bentham, which, set alongside the philosophies of James and John Stuart Mill, laid the foundations of the forms of liberal individualism so familiar to us today. The Felicific Calculus – the principle of the greatest happiness of the greatest number – was among the first philosophical statements to equate happiness with hedonism, defining happiness as pleasure devoid of pain. It replaced the Aristotelian notion of 'eudemonia', which in ancient times had equated the idea of happiness with virtue and the good life, as well as medieval notions of 'hap', meaning fate or fortune, from which etymological roots of the modern English word are derived, and which persist in expressions such as 'happenstance', 'haphazard' and ubiquitously 'perhaps'.[7] In 'Blissed Out', Connor argues that while we live in a world in which the means for the production of pleasure are abundant, we have no way of conceptualising, quantifying, or indeed, managing it. This could be a paradox, Connor argues, because part of pleasure may well involve the pleasure of the difficulty with pleasure, and indeed, the pleasures of calculation itself.

The contributors to 'Philosophical Engagements', part one of the collection, dealt with happiness in the broadest sense of the philosophical. In 'Social Interrogations', the second section of the collection, the authors turn their attention to the cultural work that happiness performs in shaping our perceptions about our lives. The discrepancy between images of happiness and the reality of lived experience is explored in Camilla Nelson's 'Happy Housewives and Angry Feminists', in which Nelson tackles one of the most startling findings of the social scientific research on happiness – the idea that children only ever bring you misery. Nelson interrogates many of the popular concep-tions of contemporary parenting, which – despite or perhaps even because of the rise of feminism – increasingly reinforce a set of impossible and contradictory ideals to which mothers feel they must aspire. Nelson highlights the mismatch between popular images of maternal bliss and the reality of the hard work of parenting, in which decisions are inevitably fretful and uneasy, and often beset by the 'dirty little secret' that the pleasures of mothers and children do not invariably coincide. Rather than embrace a model of happiness that relegates motherhood to misery, Nelson calls for a move beyond what she calls the 'thinned out notions of happiness' associated with liberal individualism, towards a more textured and communitarian understanding of happiness, that is capable of encompassing uncomfortable concepts such as pain and denial of self, but can also bring meaning and joy to life.

In his chilling essay, 'The Forest or the Pit?', David Ritter expands the horizon of what it means to be happy in the present age, by offering some stark propositions for the future: specifically, that the happy, prosperous society which we inhabit in the West has been made possible by the large-scale exploitation and consumption of fossil fuels and that happiness as we know it is therefore in jeopardy with the prospect of global warming. Ritter frames his argument with a poignant picture of the Leard Blockade, led by dedicated local and global activists intent on resisting the destruction of vast areas of state forest in order to make place for what is perhaps destined to become Australia's biggest ever open-cut coal mine, the government-supported Whitehaven Coal project adjacent to Maules Creek.

Environment sustainability is also a focus for J. K. Gibson-Graham, Jenny Cameron and Stephen Healy, whose essay, 'Pursuing Happiness: the Politics of Surviving Well Together', similarly foregrounds the need to rethink Western notions of happiness, by retrieving them from what they call the 'tyrannical demand to enjoy and to consume'. Happiness, they argue, needs to be reconstructed via a more ecological focus on the idea of 'surviving well together'. In this essay, the authors interrogate the range of economic tools that have so far been designed to measure happiness, and even the idea of measuring itself, proposing a new 'relational metrics' of happiness that is capable of encompassing both individual and planetary well-being.

In '#100HappyDays', James Arvanitakis questions the value of much of what we read and watch on happiness and self-help, attempting to rethink happiness so that it ceases to be part of the problem, and becomes part of the solution. In face of other pressing pursuits such as the need to resolve problems of poverty, the refugee crisis, war, global inequality and injustice, Arvanitakis nevertheless invokes the need for happy moments – for a new kind of happiness that grows, like Norman Lindsay's magic pudding, in the cracks and crevices of our everyday existence.

The work of reconstructing happiness is also performed in Tony Moore's essay on Australian satire and humour, in which he argues for the importance of cultural subversion in the maintenance of political and social well-being. In 'Stop Laughing – This Is Serious', Moore chronicles the often controversial career of the Australian larrikin, from the antics of Melbourne's Marcus Clarke, through Barry Humphries, to Chris Lilley's more recent comic creations. In place of an idea of happiness that might be interpreted as a form of quiescence – an injunction to do nothing, to accept or be grateful – Moore figures a politically subversive form of happiness based upon Mikhail Bakhtin's idea of the Carnivalesque, a rambunctious form of happiness that promotes both laughter and social and cultural change.

And what might literature tell us about human happiness? Deborah Pike delves into the richness of the nineteenth-century Russian novel to see what wisdom it has to offer. Pike begins her exploration by considering how complex it is for human beings to make choices which make them happy, particularly in the domain of love. Examining how difficult moral dilemmas play out in the novels of Pushkin, Tolstoy and Dostoyevsky, Pike reveals how deeply suspicious these writers are about the idea of happiness; showing that making choices based on happy feelings can lead to peril, and advocating a broader notion of human flourishing that entails the practice of virtue and connection with family and community.

In 'And They All Lived Happily Ever After', the last essay in this section, Georgina Ledvinka and Anna Kamaralli explore Western society's seemingly insatiable craving for stories with happy endings, and the way in which this desire has shaped popular cultural productions from Hollywood's appetite for blockbusters and rom-coms to the sugar-coated tales we read to our children. With a focus on children's literature, Ledvinka and Kamaralli examine how romantic notions of childhood have shaped our current understanding of who children are, and what is good for them, and how the need to keep them 'innocent' is often at odds with the reality of lived experience, as young people emerge from childhood to become citizens of the future.

'Personal Encounters', the third section of this book, examines happiness through self-reflection and via the lens of memory, investigating the ways in which personal writings and story-telling may offer more complex ways of understanding and disturbing ideas about happiness. The essays in this section include narratives of hope, sorrow and pain, and are replete with the shadowed nuances that these emotions can give to the idea of happiness. What happens when our subjective experiences and memories are put into language? How might we understand ourselves as these acts of remembering change? In 'After Zero', Alice Pung reflects on the lives of her parents, survivors of Cambodia's 'Killing Fields' and Pol Pot's Year Zero, as they rebuild their lives in a new country. Pung reinvigorates Buddha's notion of *pali* – that is, discontent – and draws attention to a richer kind of happiness, one that not only accepts the reality of suffering, but also the importance of appreciating small mercies and moments of joy. According to Pung, Western Buddhists don't like the focus on *dukkha*, or suffering, in much the same way that positive psychology does not like to focus on negative emotions. 'In this new, developed, comfortable and secure world in which my parents brought me up', writes Pung, 'it appears that we are trying to eliminate all traces of suffering'. Happiness based on the denial of suffering seems a strange and nebulous quest.

In her essay, 'On the Cancer Ward', oncologist Ranjana Srivastava also offers a nuanced understanding of happiness, as she contemplates the death of a young mother she has treated as a patient, and the lengths to which a parent will go to safeguard the well-being of her children. She writes, '[t]he consideration of happiness then leads to the perennial question of who deserves to be happy. If we make our own happiness, then what did my young patient do to 'unmake' hers?' Srivastava entertains the idea that happiness may well equate with health, and simply 'avoiding the fate' of her patients. However, having witnessed the bravery of many of her terminally ill patients Srivastava observes that although good health should never be taken for granted, life must also be celebrated through simple pleasures such as community and family.

Larissa Behrendt, like Alice Pung, offers a fresh cultural perspective on the experience of happiness. In 'The Things You Shouldn't Say to an Aboriginal Person', Behrendt explores her relationship with the Aboriginal women of her community, and highlights the importance of laughter in transcending difficult circumstances. She contemplates an idea of happiness not as catharsis, a warding off of pain, but as an experience that is richer and deeper, involving warmth, inclusion, storytelling and the forging of social bonds; these provide a more authentic sense of contentment. Happiness may begin with laughter, but it also thrives in an awareness of the world around, in song, music and dance. For Aboriginal people, it also means self-determination and commitment to a goal which will make life better for everyone.

This book does not attempt to discard the idea of happiness, but to think of it in new and more socially attuned ways. It is not written in a spirit of cynical disillusion, or with an attachment to suffering as a shiny badge of wisdom or intelligence. On the contrary, the editors would like to see more smiles and more laughter – to engender new ideas and theories of happiness, from developing communities, to ensuring peaceful relationships, to gaining material security, to self-realisation and exploiting one's talents, to practising virtue, to being healthy, to living with novelty and stimulation, to caring for our planet, to cultivating an atmosphere of growth and learning, to striving and goal-setting, to developing and maintaining a spiritual life, and yes, to hugging more than five people a day.

Endnotes

1   B. Ehrenreich, *Smile or Die: How Positive Thinking Fooled America and the World*, Granta Publications, London, 2010, pp. 15–44.

2   A. Sen, *Development as Freedom*, Oxford University Press, Oxford and New York, 2001.

3   M. Nussbaum, 'Who is the happy warrior? Philosophy Poses Questions to Psychology', *Journal of Legal Studies*, vol. 37, no. S2, 2008, pp. 81–113; and 'Who is the Happy Warrior? Philosophy, Happiness Research, and Public Policy', *International Review of Economics*, vol. 59, no. 4, 2012, pp. 335–61.

4   K. Vonnegut, *A Man Without a Country*, Seven Stories Press, New York, 2011, p. 6.

5   The theory that wages don't relate to happiness is known as the Easterlin Paradox. See R. Easterlin, 'Does economic growth improve the human lot? Some empirical evidence', in P. A. David and M. W. Reder (eds), *Nations and Households in Economic Growth: Essays in Honor of Moses Abramovitz*, Academic Press, New York, 1974, pp. 89–125.

6   The most cited study alleging that parents report statistically significant lower levels of happiness than nonparents was authored by the Nobel Prize–winning behavioural economist Daniel Kahneman. See, D. Kahneman, A. B. Krueger, D. A. Schkade, N. Schwarz, & A. A. Stone (2004). 'A survey method for characterizing daily life experience: The day reconstruction method', *Science*, vol. 306. no. 5702, pp. 1776–80. This has been supported by numerous further studies including a recent British survey of more than 4,000 people carried out by the Open University. See J. Gabb, M. Klett-Davies, J. Fink & M. Thomae, 'Enduring Love? Couple Relationships in the 21st Century', Survey Report Findings, Open University, 2013.

7   On the history of the idea of happiness see D. McMahon, *Happiness, a History*, Atlantic Monthly Press, New York, 2006.

1

PHILOSOPHICAL ENGAGEMENTS

THE LIES OF HAPPINESS

Clive Hamilton

In a short story titled 'Grief' Anton Chekhov tells of a wood-turner named Grigory Petrov, a drunkard, bully and layabout who regularly beat his wife for forty years. One night he arrives home drunk and brandishing his fists. This time, instead of shrinking from him, his wife gazes at him sternly, 'as saints do from their icons', wrote Chekhov.

It was her first and last act of defiance.

Now driving a sled through a blizzard, Petrov is taking his dying wife to the doctor. He curses and whips the horse. He is seized by grief for a life wasted, and wonders how he will live without this woman who has sustained him for so long. I may have been a drunkard and ne'er-do-well, he mutters to himself, but that was never the true man, and now my wife is dying on me, she will never know my better nature. I beat her, it's true, but never out of spite. Am I not now rushing her to the doctor because I feel sorry for her?

In Chekhov's story, Petrov engages in grotesque rationalisations. His dignity will not allow him to face the truth of the sort of man he is. He engages in a litany of self-deceptions, even though at every step of the old horse the truth threatens to overwhelm him.

The myriad ways humans lie to themselves is one of the recurring themes of literature. Because we all engage in self-deception, we recognise ourselves in the characters. We are forever composing stories about ourselves and our world so as to smooth a path through life.

The psychologist Shelley Taylor calls them 'benign fictions'. They are the lies we deploy to defend our happiness. For a long time I have believed that if we deceive ourselves about our strengths and weaknesses, creating a veil that distorts our vision of the world so as to render it more agreeable, we may actually be sacrificing the opportunity to find a more authentic self from which to live. But is that chasing a phantom? Does it really matter if we find contentment by deploying benign fictions?

The philosophers have always told us that happiness should be discounted if it floats on a mirage of lies. But maybe the thinkers are deceiving themselves, rationalising away their melancholy and inflating the value of their solemnity.

Perhaps. Yet there is another reason to question happiness built on self-deception. It opens us up to manipulation. When we are not truthful with ourselves, we are driven by forces of which we are unconscious, but our real motives and desires can be discerned by others – advertisers, for instance. They can smell weaknesses to be exploited.

So, I am willing to argue, those whose happiness rests on fabrications risk surrendering their freedom. Happiness at the price of freedom is not worth it, unless the limits to one's freedom are freely chosen after careful reflection.

The other day I caught a snippet of conversation as I passed two young women sitting on a bench. One said to the other,

'He knows deep down...'. That's all. We all know what she meant: the man in question is deceiving himself in some way. Perhaps he 'knows deep down' that his marriage is doomed, but refuses to accept that his partner loves him no more. Perhaps he 'knows deep down' that it is wrong to cheat on his tax return, but tells himself that he pays plenty of tax and doesn't everyone cheat?

Anna Freud, Sigmund's daughter, developed the idea of defence mechanisms that enable us to conceal uncomfortable truths from ourselves. We push these truths into the unconscious and the task of the analyst is to bring them back to the surface. So when we engage in *repression* we exclude certain memories, feelings or associations that would be upsetting if consciously acknowledged. In short, we act as if we are unaware of some fact that is apparent to others.

Use of these mechanisms is never deliberate. If it were, they would have no effect. The tension between the conscious attitude and the deeper emotion will manifest itself somehow, if only through a vague feeling that something is not right. If the feeling is strong enough it may ultimately compel us to face up to the truth, whatever the pain it may cause.

But is the truth always to be preferred?

The Trade Practices Act outlaws deceptive and misleading conduct by companies making claims about their products. But what if we *want* to believe the lies? It is the essence of branding that by identifying ourselves deeply with a brand – an Apple computer, Diesel clothing, a Volvo car – we take on the image associated with it. We accept these commercially provided identities because our societies no longer offer other means of creating a sense of self that satisfies. And we are bored.

Increasingly, our attention is seen as a scarce commodity. As always, anything that is scarce has a value, and some are willing to pay for it. There is even a new branch of economics called 'attention economics'. When information is thrust on us by others it can be regarded as a form of pollution. We sometimes try to stop this pollution harming us with devices such as spam blockers, television mute buttons, 'Do not call' registers and 'No junk mail' stickers. However, I think many of us watch television and listen to iPods to avoid paying attention to aspects of our lives that are uncomfortable. And we *want* our attention to be captured because we have developed a strong aversion to boredom. It seems to me that the flight from boredom means our society as a whole is suffering from a form of attention deficit hyperactivity disorder (ADHD). Movies and television programs have shorter scenes and more action in order to keep us 'glued to the set'. Yet in order to transcend boredom it is necessary to get beneath the superficial self that is entertained by television and a thousand other distractions.

It is banal to observe that one of the most common forms of self-deception today is the belief that by having more money and owning more things our lives will be happier. Our entire political-economic system would collapse if it were not for this grandest of all lies. A vast marketing industry exists in order to create dissatisfaction, to manufacture the wants essential for the system to reproduce itself.

The evidence that, above a certain level, more money does not bring more happiness comes in two forms. First, a swag of psychological studies has separated out the factors that distinguish happy people from unhappy ones. The researchers initially classified individuals according to whether they value and pursue extrinsic goals (money, fame and beauty) or intrinsic goals (relationships and personal growth). They then asked which group is happier. The results are summarised by Tim Kasser in *The High Price of Materialism*. 'Individuals oriented towards materialistic, extrinsic goals are more likely to experience lower quality of life than individuals oriented toward intrinsic goals'. Not only are those with extrinsic orientation in life less happy than those with intrinsic goals, they make others less happy too. Their relationships are more competitive and plagued by conflict, so they are shorter. Nevertheless, these extrinsic goals are the ones officially sanctioned and relentlessly promoted in consumer society.

The second type of evidence arises in our own lives. Frequently, when our wishes for more money or a bigger house are fulfilled, they do not bring the contentment we expected. We may reconcile ourselves to these 'disconfirmed expectations' by telling ourselves that we obviously bought the wrong thing, but will not make the same mistake again. Or we may choose to believe others who say we must be happier now that we have a bigger house. Most people believe that our society is too focused on money and material things, but very few believe that they themselves are too materialistic. Most people believe that advertising is very effective at changing people's behaviour, but they are convinced that they personally are not affected by it. We know advertising is full of claims that are often absurd, so to admit to being influenced by it seems to be an admission of gullibility and simple-mindedness. More deeply, we need to believe in our own free will. Believing in our own autonomy is fundamental to the sense of self in modern Western societies. No-one wants to admit, least of all to themselves, that they are being manipulated. Yet embracing the fiction that we are immune to persuasion means we are collaborating in the advertisers' attempts to manipulate us with their sophisticated technology of happiness.

Admitting that we are vulnerable to the marketers' tactics, and to the broader money culture, may be the first step to attaining real freedom. For then we can truly question what it is in us that is being seduced by marketing. Until we own up to it, we cannot control it. Only then can we become conscious consumers. Then if we buy something because it appeals to our vanity or exploits an insecurity, at least we will be doing so honestly.

The extent to which we deceive ourselves about money is curious because the belief in the power of money is often only skin deep. We don't have to delve far into people's beliefs before realising that most people understand that money does not buy happiness because the sort of happiness money can buy is not 'the real thing'. Although their conduct may appear to belie it, few people genuinely believe that life should be pursued as a sequence of positive affects – maximising the number and duration of emotional and physical highs and minimising the lows. Those who do believe this usually turn to drugs or to forms of compulsive behaviour – including money-hunger – in order to keep the desired combination of brain chemicals flowing.

Most Australians realise this is the road to perdition.

There have been scores of surveys asking about levels of happiness, but a more interesting and pregnant result emerged from a survey I commissioned a few years ago in which Australians were asked whether they would be willing occasionally to take a drug that made them happy if it were legally available and free of side effects. Remarkably almost three-quarters of Australians said they would *not* take a legally available happiness drug, even occasionally.

Why, in the midst of societies in which hedonism is so strongly and consistently encouraged and practised, do such large majorities of Australians reject the idea of taking a pill in order to attain happiness? This question goes to the heart of how people understand their lives, a deep-seated if rarely articulated belief that a worthwhile life requires authentic engagement with the world around us, including relationships with others. Real life involves difficult challenges and painful mistakes and taking a happiness pill would be a 'cop-out'. The story of the happiness pill has redemptive value, and points to a deeper propensity for reflection than the public has been credited with. Rejecting guaranteed cheer makes the citizen, or at least the three-quarters who said they would not take the pill, more akin to Aristotle than the hedonist of the economics textbooks.

But I think the fracture in modern consumer societies goes deeper. It is one thing to recognise that money and the consumer life are in some way shallow; it is quite another to find out what a more 'authentic' life would be. Sometimes I doubt whether there can be such a thing in our secular societies and that we are destined to live out selves wholly given to us by the social conditions in which we find ourselves. Still, there must be some identity more authentic than those constructed for us by the clever manipulators who make brands and produce popular culture. At a minimum, we must fight hard against those influences, for if we do not we will end up as mere ciphers.

Creating the illusion of independence is the most potent tool of the contemporary advertisers' trade, but the irony is generally lost because most people are too busy congratulating themselves on 'being their own person'. The essential ideology of modern consumerism is that we can all live freely and independently. This is an idea that emerged from the ideal marriage of modern consumerism and the ideology of the liberation movements of the 1960s and 1970s, and which we now hear expressed in inane phrases such as 'be true to yourself' and 'you are responsible for your own happiness'. So instead of pledging allegiance to God, nowadays a Girl Guide in Britain promises to be 'true to myself', a vapid vow that nevertheless resonates with the inherent nihilism of individualised societies.

In Australia over the last thirteen or fourteen years we have engaged in a national conversation about happiness and how to get it, in large part stimulated by the work of my former colleagues at the Australia Institute, building on the writings of Richard Eckersley. From the early 2000s we asked whether national well-being was rising along with rates of economic growth. We found that the answer was 'no'. We built the Genuine Progress Indicator as a substitute for GDP. We showed how advertisers were persuading us to go into debt and how they were increasingly targeting children. We pointed to an epidemic of overwork and estimated that a third of Sydney fathers spend more time in their cars commuting than at home playing with their children. We measured the value of the stuff we buy and then throw out unused (billions of dollars worth). We pointed out that Australians spend more on pet food than on foreign aid. We entertained radio listeners with stories of $7,000 barbecues. We calculated that while Australian households were shrinking in size the houses they live in were becoming bigger. And we tracked the growth of a bizarre new profession known as 'declutterers' who give advice on how to rid one's house of stuff. In short, we challenged the frenzy of the consumer boom – captured in the obsession with house prices – by posing a simple question: Is all that materialism actually making you happy?

We discovered a deep vein of discontent – with oppressive levels of debt, marriages under stress, overwork leading to illness and depression, children being neglected and a pervasive anomie. And then we uncovered the reaction against it all by describing the remarkably large numbers who had decided to downshift, that is, to voluntarily reduce their incomes and consumption in order to take back some control over their lives. My colleague Richard Denniss and I put it all together in a popular book, *Affluenza: When too much is never enough*, which has sold more than 40,000 copies and still provokes a trickle of emails saying 'thank you, you changed my life'.

For a time we succeeded in provoking some deep questioning in the community, but then something happened. The 2008 global financial crisis brought the Zeitgeist to a sudden end and the happiness debate evaporated. The crash was the direct result of excessive consumption, unsustainable debt and the expansion of the industries that made them possible; in other words, everything we had criticised.

I always saw the happiness debate we triggered as no more than a prelude to the real task of opening people up to an examination of some deeper sense of meaning in their lives, and to precipitate reflection on the moral basis and behavioural structure of our society. These questions about the meaning and purpose of human life have occupied philosophers for thousands of years, and it is apparent that – despite the spread of affluence, instant gratification and contingent relationships – many Australians today would agree, at least in principle, with John Stuart Mill when he wrote, 'It is…better to be Socrates dissatisfied than a fool satisfied'.

Yet, here we are, in the embryonic stages of the next consumer boom, seemingly with no collective lessons learned from the last one.

Most people continue to act as if money buys happiness because in our society money has become the principal means of obtaining what we all crave – *recognition*. This is particularly true in the business sector and for those who perch on the higher limbs of the corporate tree. The belief that our worth is measured by the amount of money we earn explains why many businesses prefer that their employees do not know how much their peers earn – if we find they earn more, we feel devalued. It also explains the extraordinary inflation in executive salaries in recent years. Shareholders are said to have a right to know how much their CEOs are being paid, but when the law was changed requiring corporations to publish details of executive remuneration in their annual reports, CEOs discovered how much their rivals at other corporations were earning. As salaries are the measure of status, an executive salary arms race was set in train. Public outrage over a multimillion dollar annual pay cheque does not shame the recipient into asking for less; on the contrary, it only enhances his reputation among his peers.

In societies or subcultures that have nonpecuniary means of conferring recognition, money's importance shrinks. In the academic community the admiration of one's peers derives from the ability to have one's papers published in prestigious journals, so the fact that many academics could earn much more else-where has little relevance. Whether status, beyond recognition, brings happiness is a subtler question. Perhaps it does, although the pursuit of status can prompt counterproductive behaviours. Self-importance is one of the primary manifestations of self-deception. We habitually observe individuals inflating their status in their own minds. We comfort ourselves with the old saw that pride comes before the fall. Yet pride often endures, undeflated, sustained by the endless capacity to deceive.

Mr Collins, the pompous and unprepossessing clergyman in *Pride and Prejudice*, is convinced he would be a very good catch for Miss Elizabeth Bennet. When Elizabeth refuses his pro-posal, the clergyman is undeterred. It is only when Elizabeth's father, at his daughter's insistence, refuses on her behalf that Mr Collins accepts the truth, or at least half of it. So convinced is he that no-one in Elizabeth's position could refuse his proposal, accepting her rejection demands either a radical revision of his own self-concept or an attack on the character of Lizzie. So he interprets Miss Bennet's rejection as a sign not of his personal flaws but of hers, of her vanity and willful refusal to recognise what is in her own interest. Although the reader understands that Mr Collins is deceiving himself, he believes that it is in fact

Lizzie who is deluded. Of course, Austen understood that we are never more prone to misleading ourselves than in matters of love. Yet there is no love between Mr Collins and Miss Bennet. It is pride that deceives, in the same way that contestants who fail auditions for *Australian Idol* storm out denouncing the judges as fools.

But who am I to condemn the benign fictions of others? My own rise up before me.

Perhaps the archetypal modern man is not Mr Collins, but David Brent, the emotionally tone-deaf and deluded boss of *The Office*. For many men, Brent, with his carapace of self-delusion, is the last man they would want to be; yet he is undeniably the happiest man in the office. Perhaps the quest for this thing called authenticity is quixotic, and the life-course of the happy idiot has more to recommend it.

WHAT HAPPINESS CONCEALS

John Quiggin

There has, over the past couple of decades, been a remarkable boom in economic research into happiness. Strangely enough, it might have originated in remarks made in the early 1970s by Jigme Singye Wangchuck at the time of his coronation as absolute monarch of Bhutan, one of the poorest countries on earth. Questioned about policies to promote growth in Gross National Product, the King said he would rather strive to promote Gross National Happiness than the conventional goal of Gross National Product. This neat aphorism spurred on a full-scale research agenda, not only in Bhutan but in the developed world as well. Over time, a new group of academic stars – if not household names – has emerged, not least economists such as Richard Easterlin, Bruno Frey and Richard Layard.

And what have we learnt so far? Chiefly this: that there is a reason why everyone reads Dante's 'Inferno' and no-one reads his 'Paradiso'. 'All happy families are alike', Tolstoy wrote; he might have added that this is why so few of them appear in novels. Maybe there just isn't anything interesting to say about happiness. That certainly seems true of the social-science work on it, where even the most basic results look like shadows cast by the analytical framework rather than genuine discoveries.

Popular Now

Take the field's crucial finding, the so-called Easterlin paradox. Cross-country data seem to show pretty consistently that, on average, happiness increases with income, but only up to a certain point.[1] In the developed world, for example, people are scarcely happier than they were in the 1960s. The evidence for this claim consists of surveys in which people rate their happiness on a scale, typically from one to ten. Within any given society, happiness tends to rise with all the obvious variables: income, health, family relationships and so on. But between societies, or in Western societies such as Australia over time, there's not much movement, even though both income and health have improved pretty steadily for a long time.

This sounds like quite a discovery: happiness is relative! But in fact the result is probably an illusion. To see why, just consider this puzzle. Suppose you wanted to establish whether children's height increased with age, but for some reason you couldn't measure them directly. One way to start the investigation would be to interview groups of children in different classes at school and ask them the question: 'On a scale of one to ten, how tall are you?' You'd find that kids who were old relative to their classmates would tend to report higher numbers than those who were young relative to their classmates. After all, the older ones would mostly be taller than the younger ones. So far, so good.

After you had surveyed a few classes, you might start to notice something rather odd. As you moved up through the year groups, the average age would keep increasing but the average reported height would not change much. For all age groups, the median response would be something like seven (accounting for the 'Lake Wobegon' effect, by which nearly everyone thinks of themselves as above average). What to make of that?

By analogy with the 'happiness puzzle', you might conclude that height is a subjective construct depending on relative, rather than absolute, age. But, in reality, we know that height actually does increase with age throughout childhood. The problem is that asking for a subjective mark out of ten is a silly way to measure height. Each child is likely to score himself relative to his classmates rather than to any absolute scale, with the result that comparisons between age groups are meaningless. Does happiness keep rising with income? Nobody can say. But, since we don't have any absolute scale of mood, it certainly seems plausible that people judge it in pretty much the same way as the children judged height in our imaginary investigation.

In a society where most people are hungry most of the time, having a full belly might justify a pretty decent happiness score. If everyone has enough to eat but it's mostly rice or potatoes, you might consider yourself blessed to be eating roast chicken, and so on. The objective level of income and health needed to report yourself as more than averagely happy will depend on what you consider average. This is true whether or not people in rich societies are in fact happier, and whether or not the average person is happier now than the average person in 1960. A relative scale tells us nothing one way or the other. And as far as happiness goes, a relative scale seems to be all that we can hope for.

Economists are famous for concentrating on problems for which they have data, rather than ones that matter. As an old joke has it, they are like the drunk man searching for his keys under a lamppost because the light is better there. So: happiness is intrinsically shadowy. Indeed, according to the so-called 'hedonic paradox', even those who hope to achieve it in their own lives can approach it only indirectly. As John Stuart Mill observed in 1873: 'Aiming thus at something else, they find happiness by the way [...] Ask yourself whether you are happy, and you cease to be so'.

Misery, by contrast, is a marvellously rich source of data. Unhappy families are, as Tolstoy pointed out, much more varied than happy ones. And if happiness is elusive and subjective, there are plenty of objective sources of unhappiness: hunger, illness, the premature death of loved ones, family breakdown and so on. We can measure the ways these things change over time and compare that data to subjective emotional evidence. A whole new research program suggests itself.

When we shift our attention from unhappiness, some important political distinctions also come to light. Broadly speaking, everyone is in favour of happiness. It is a classic 'motherhood' issue (more so, indeed, than motherhood). Utilitarians seek to maximise it, even if they no longer believe in the precision of Jeremy Bentham's 'felicific calculus'. The classical liberals who wrote the US Declaration of Independence listed the pursuit of it among the inalienable rights of (white) men. Conservatives, according to a large body of scientific research, claim to be happier than liberals (in both the US and the European sense of 'liberal'). Even the Nazis sought 'strength through joy'. Of course, different political viewpoints yield different claims about what is most likely to promote happiness, but pretty much everyone is in favour of it. Even a book such as Eric Wilson's *Against Happiness* (2008) turns out to be more accurately described by its subtitle: 'In Praise of Melancholy'.

Unhappiness, by contrast, is divisive. Utilitarians take the common-sense view that, just as happiness is good and to be promoted, unhappiness is bad and should be minimised. This idea, coupled with the belief that the state should act to relieve unhappiness, is central to the philosophy of social democrats (and, with some qualifications, social liberals). The political right, by contrast, has a more equivocal view of unhappiness. Just consider the central dividing line of modern politics: welfare.

As an institution, the welfare state is not traditionally associated with very much happiness. If asked to list the sources of joy in our lives, few of us would include the receipt of unemployment benefits or a stay in a public hospital. But what it does (or tries to do) is minimise the sources of unhappiness in a market economy. It addresses illness, loss of income through unemployment or inability to work, homelessness and so on. This is not to say that, even in the most comprehensive system – one in which the fear of unemployment has been banished and there are decent public services for all – everyone is happy. Money doesn't buy happiness. Still, as the comedian Spike Milligan said, it does buy a better class of unhappiness.

And as far as that goes, the welfare state has had a remarkable track record. You just have to compare outcomes in nations that have modern welfare systems with those in the US, where the New Deal produced only stunted versions of the standard institutions. American technology leads the world and the US constitution endorses the pursuit of happiness. Yet on numerous important development indices, including premature mortality, food security, incarceration and access to health care, the US lags behind much of the rest of the developed world. For many Americans, a better class of unhappiness would do nicely.

Despite its achievements, the welfare state has never won much love on the political right. Why is that? Ostensibly, the chief point in the right-wing critique is that it creates more misery than it relieves in the long run. This argument generally depends on claims about the adverse incentive effects of high taxes and welfare payments – claims that have not, in general, stood up very well to data. The literature on these topics is huge, but perhaps the most striking evidence is the plummeting proportion of adult Americans who are in work, despite the supposedly powerful incentives of low taxes and minimal welfare.

Underlying ostensibly practical objections however, we often find signs of a belief that unhappiness is actually good for us, or at least, good for those on whom it is imposed. This idea might draw support from the orthodox Christian vision of the present world as a vale of tears in which original sin must be expiated. More generally, conservatives frequently see unhappiness as both inevitable, given the futility of attempts to reform human nature, and a necessary part of building an upright character.

William Bennett, a representative figure, served as US education secretary during the Reagan administration. In *The Book of Virtues: A Treasury of Great Moral Stories* (1993), which he edited, Bennett finds the greatness of American character exemplified by (at least some of) the members of the Donner Party, a group of nineteenth-century pioneers who got trapped by snow in the Sierra Nevada. Many of them starved to death. Others survived only by eating the remains of their companions. As you might expect, the situation brought out both the best and the worst in people. But Bennett's wistful admiration of the stoic survivors as paragons from a more virtuous age ('Where did those people go?' he wonders) shows just how deep the division is between conservative 'virtue ethics' and the consequentialist view that unhappiness is an evil to be minimised. Bertolt Brecht sums up this division neatly in his play *Galileo* (1943), meeting the virtue-ethicist line 'Unhappy the land that has no heroes!' with a consequentialist riposte: 'No. Unhappy is the land that needs a hero'.

If traditional conservatives speak highly of unhappiness, an even rosier view can be found among Prometheans and radicals of both the right and left. For market liberals, for example, the idea that we could ever be satisfied with a given level of material comfort is anathema. Our unhappiness with what we have is exactly what makes us strive for more. The market economy that makes this possible therefore represents the highest possible stage of social evolution.

The American political writer Virginia Postrel is a particularly eloquent advocate for this system of insatiable desire. She has argued against broadly instrumentalist theories of conspicuous consumption that claim we seek luxuries in order to impress others and pursue social status. In Postrel's view, consumers will seek luxury even in items that no-one else will ever see, such as $400 toilet brushes. Her book *The Power of Glamour* (2013) presents glamour as a kind of 'nonverbal rhetoric' that 'leads us to feel that the life we dream of exists, and to desire it even more'.

Unlike merely material needs, the need for glamour can never be assuaged. For the vast majority of us, the prize must remain forever out of reach. Nevertheless, Postrel argues, we are better off striving after what we know to be illusions than living with the dull contentment we find when our objective material needs are satisfied. (Those who starve while others dissipate resources in the pursuit of glamour might have a different view.)

And it is only fair to note that not all of the champions of unhappiness are on the political right. Some on the Marxist left have argued that, like religion, social welfare is an opiate for the masses. By dulling the pain of poverty and unemployment, both welfare and religion diminish the anger that workers ought to feel at a system that exploits and alienates them. The revolutionary alternative would be to 'heighten the contradictions' of capitalism – by making it more miserable, until it is no longer tolerable.

For a brief moment in the 1960s, it appeared that this radical critique might succeed. A (largely hypothetical) alliance of downtrodden workers and postmaterialist student radicals would shatter the illusion of prosperous middle-class consensus and dispense with the palliatives of the welfare system, calling forth a new society in which genuine happiness for all might finally flourish.

In fact, this left-wing revolt achieved little except weakening the defences of the welfare state against the real challenge, which came from the free-market right. Nevertheless, a good deal of social criticism draws on the residual appeal of this critique, denouncing any ameliorative reform while implicitly conceding that there is nothing else on offer. One group that has taken this line to its logical conclusion is the former Revolutionary Communist Party of the UK, most of whose members are now associated with the market-libertarian group around *Spiked* magazine.

We are now at something of an impasse. Despite decades of pressure for cutbacks and rationalisation, the core institutions of the welfare state have endured. In most countries, what protects them is a sense on the part of the public that they are the only reliable bulwark against the miseries of unemployment, ill health and old age. Yet welfare's opponents remain, and they are often, as we have seen, ideologically wedded to various forms of unhappiness, at least as experienced by others.

So, perhaps we need a new research program, to examine how unhappiness really works. Does hunger, or unemployment, or the loss of a family member to preventable illness make you a stronger and better person? Is striving after more and better possessions more fulfilling than satisfaction with what you have? It's obvious from the way I've posed these questions what I believe the answer to be. But genuine research into the economics of unhappiness might yield some surprising answers to such questions as these, and reveal new questions that we have never before considered.

Perhaps Bhutan will lead the way once again. Paternalist monarchy has given way to democratic elections, the second of which produced a surprise win for the People's Democratic Party of Tshering Tobgay in 2013. Tellingly, he has abandoned the pursuit of Gross National Happiness. 'Rather than talking about happiness,' Tobgay told the *New York Times*, 'we want to work on reducing the obstacles to happiness'. Such a pragmatic view might not make Tobgay a cultural icon like his predecessor, but it seems likely to do more to relieve the people of Bhutan from the various miseries attendant on poverty.

Endnotes

1   Other researchers, such as Justin Wolfers and Betsey Stevenson, using different measures of happiness, have found a statistically significant, but relatively small, link between increased income and self-reported happiness over time.

LOVING HAPPINESS BUT FEELING SAD

Brock Bastian

Imagine for a moment that you have decided you would like a new car. You have seen it advertised, a few of your friends have bought one, and it seems like it will suit you really well. You start to save for your car, each day you put away a little bit more money. At the end of six months you hope that you have enough, but on inspection of your bank account you realise you are still short. This gap between how much money you would like to have, so you could buy your car, and the amount of money that you actually do have makes you feel disappointed. In time however you manage to turn your disappointment into new found motivation and start to save again, eventually meeting your goal and buying your dream car.

Now, imagine that instead of a car your goal is to be happy. You work on this each day, trying to become a little bit happier than you were before. At the end of six months you sit down and assess whether you are as happy as you had aimed to be. You realise that actually you had hoped to be happier than you actually are (how were you to know that you would experience a relationship breakdown, lose your job, and fall out with your parents?). This gap between how much happiness you would like to have, and how happy you actually are, makes you feel disappointed. Now, as disappointment is a negative emotion, over time this starts to interfere with your levels of happiness. In fact, in contrast to your goal to feel happy, much of the time you start to feel disappointed about how unhappy you are. Eventually you realise that not only are you less happy than you had aimed to be, but you are less happy than you were when you hatched this masterful plan!

This example illustrates that trying to be happy can often, and perhaps most often, be counterproductive at best and out-right damaging at worst. It also illustrates the reason why one of the most powerful strategies for achieving happiness is to give up trying to be happy. The very act of trying to be happy ironically pushes happiness further away. Indeed it seems that it is in contexts where people most expect to be happy that they are ironically least able to achieve this emotional state.[1] This also suggests that simply focusing on happiness may not be the best way to build a good life, and seeking out meaning in life – which may be derived from both positive and negative experiences – seems to have better prospects when it comes to maximising what the Ancient Greeks called 'eudemonia' or human flourishing.

The Cost of Loving Happiness

These insights hold important implications for how we should seek to promote happiness. The positive psychology move-ment was launched over a decade ago by Martin Seligman and colleagues and in its application the importance of positive experiences, positive mindsets, and positive emotions for well-being and performance have often been championed. This has been a resounding success and indeed positive emotions have been shown to have a range of positive health benefits. Yet the above analysis suggests that when too much emphasis is placed on the importance of feeling happy, when happiness is seen as a goal in and of itself, or when the pursuit of happiness becomes pressured, this may produce a number of ironic and counterproductive effects – in the end, it may actually serve to produce more sadness.

There are also other ways in which the blind pursuit of happiness may have a downside. First, it is true to say that too much happiness may not be good for us. To a modern Westerner this statement may seem internally inconsistent or just blatantly untrue – surely it is not possible to have too much of a good thing? For those accustomed to Eastern philosophy, however, the notion that there can be too much of a good thing is very familiar. In Japan for instance, emotional balance is valued more than blatant positivity and the pursuit of happiness can sometimes be viewed as 'immoral'. Early thinkers such as Aristotle likewise saw the value in balance, advocating the 'golden mean' as the most important goal for the good life. Consistent with these ideas there is now plenty of evidence to suggest that extreme levels of happiness may actually be harmful. For example, very happy people tend to engage in riskier behaviours, live shorter lives and earn lower salaries.[2] Indeed even moderately happy people may be more prejudiced[3] and tend to be less realistic in their view of the world.[4] These examples give us good reason to believe that more happiness is not always better, and endlessly promoting happiness (or promoting endless happiness) may not always be the best thing.

The second way that pursuing happiness may have a down-side is not so much to do with how people value happiness, but with the relative value they place on sadness. Although scientists interested in the study of emotion are well aware that positive and negative emotions tend to occur relatively independently of each other, this is not so much how lay people think about broad emotional concepts such as 'happiness' and 'sadness'. Rather these emotional concepts tend to be viewed as mutually exclusive – being more happy means being less sad, and being less sad means being more happy. This is why when people do not achieve their goal of happiness they experience their disappointment – a negative 'nonhappy' emotion – as a threat to that goal. Within these contexts, feelings of sadness are not only counterproductive to the experience of happiness, but they may become overlaid with values attached to success and achievement. Being happy becomes an indicator of the successful life, while being sad feels like one is a failure.

The relative devaluation of negative emotions, such as sadness, is perhaps the most sinister downside to the mindless pursuit of happiness. When sadness is viewed as a sign of failure it becomes unacceptable for people to have this experience – they find it aversive, they do not like it, and moreover they become upset about the fact that they are sad. This is perhaps why many psychologists report that the people they see for the treatment of depression are often more depressed about being depressed than they are actually just depressed. It is this negative reaction to negative emotion which is often most damaging; it is a maladaptive response that drives people further into depression. Within clinical circles, this kind of reaction is termed 'secondary disturbance' and has been the focus of treatment regimes aimed at alleviating a range of psychological disorders. These approaches attempt to help people accept their negative emotions, rather than react to them. To see them as valuable and as something that should not be feared, avoided, or, most importantly, responded to with more negative emotion. The message that feeling sad is a normal part of life is powerful. This is because when sadness is normalised, people are less likely to experience secondary disturbances (i.e. the process of getting upset about being upset) and therefore experience less sadness overall. Accepting unpleasant emotional states is an effective pathway to alleviating depression and other emotional problems.

Cultures That Love Happiness

The power of accepting negative emotion as normal has been demonstrated in psychological treatments for emotional disturbance. This is because people walk out of these sessions more willing to accept the full spectrum of their emotional experiences. What happens outside the therapist's door, however, may be an entirely different story. While psychologists are teaching people that they should be more accepting of their negative emotions, the cultures within which those people live may be sending a very different message. People are easily swayed by the normative influences of their cultures and cultural values, and customs or conventions are important determinants of an individual's emotional experience. This raises the important question of whether accepting one's own sadness may be less effective if that sadness is viewed as unacceptable and inappropriate by those around us.

It doesn't take too much to work out which emotional states are more highly valued in Westernised (and other) societies.

As Barbara Ehrenreich argues in her aptly titled book *Smile or Die*, Western culture has become obsessed with optimism and happiness. Schools aim to increase the happiness of their students, and organisations seek to maximise the happiness of their employees.[5] National campaigns are designed to promote the happiness of their constituents, and the happiness of a nation is now measured in similar ways to Gross Domestic Product. Indeed, a brief Google search will reveal a number of maps charting national differences in happiness.

Happiness is also a close bedfellow of marketing and consumerism. Can you remember the last time you saw an advertisement on television where someone looked unhappy? I would venture to suggest that the only time we see unhappiness marketed to us is when we are being informed about a new treatment for it. Be it antidepressants, painkillers, or even a new suit and nice car, we are being sent the message that the value of all these things is that they will make us happier. Underlying this kind of materialism is the basic goal to maximise pleasure and happiness through unfettered and mostly unnecessary consumption. Indeed, even happiness itself has become a commodity, with the shelves of most bookshops lined with paperbacks offering the latest perspective on how to best maximise one's levels of happiness.

This focus on the value of happiness stands in stark contrast to the ways in which sadness is valued. At best it is seen as an aberration; at worst it is pathologised and medicalised. More and more people are presenting to GPs with feelings of sadness that are being casually labelled as depression. Of course depression itself is not necessarily a pathological state, and feelings of depression can be aptly described as part of what it means to be a healthy individual. For instance, feeling depressed at the loss of one of your parents is expected, normal and even necessary. In this context it would be a failure to feel depressed or sad that would be most concerning. Nonetheless, in clinical contexts 'depression' is a term that opens the door to pharmacological and psychological treatment regimes. As such, common malaise is often diagnosed as an illness,[6] and treated with drugs and other interventions designed to quickly and efficiently return people to 'normality'. Left out of the prominent discourse in these contexts is the recognition that negative emotions may have a range of positive consequences, such as unleashing creative potential,[7] solidifying interpersonal relations,[8] and providing the foundation for a rich and meaningful life.[9]

So is living in cultures that value happiness really a bad thing? Surely it would be better to live in a place in which others like you to feel happy than one in which they would prefer that you drown in your own sadness? My colleagues and I have investigated this question, focusing on whether living in cultures that value happiness promotes a sense of satisfaction in life.[10] Looking at more than 45 countries worldwide we found that people who live in societies that value happiness are indeed more satisfied with their lives. Importantly, however, we found that this was especially the case for people who tend to experience few negative emotions. For those who tend to experience many negative emotions, this value placed on happiness is less likely to increase life satisfaction and well-being. This work suggests that cultures that love happiness may have benefits for some – those who find happiness comes easily for them – but for those who struggle to find happiness in their lives these benefits are less apparent.

Another way in which these cultures may create problems for those who *do* tend to experience negative emotions is that these individuals may feel that those around them expect them *not* to feel that way. That is, people may feel socially pressured only to experience and express positive emotion and *not* to experience or express negative emotion. In research focusing on how people respond to this perceived social pressure,[11] my colleagues and I have found that when people feel that others expect them not to experience or express sadness, they tend to experience more sadness, more depression, and are less satisfied with their lives. Furthermore, these negative responses were driven by a tendency to reflect negatively on the self when experiencing negative emotions such as sadness. We refer to this effect as 'feeling bad about being sad', a response to sadness that was more powerfully predicted by what people felt other people and their societies more generally expected of them, compared with their own personal expectations not to experience negative emotion. Our ongoing work on this topic is revealing that the perceived social pressure to be happy and not sad has a range of negative consequences, from increasing feelings of loneliness and social isolation for those who experience many negative emotional states, to dysfunctional responses to negative emotion such as rumination, and a tendency, somewhat ironically, to become more focused on negative than positive emotional information.

But Why Can't I Love Happiness?

I would be a fool if my message was to convince you to dislike happiness and love sadness. I very much doubt that you would flourish under the burden of this ill-fated advice. I for one do love to be happy, and would prefer to be happy more often than sad. That said, I doubt that I would like to be endlessly happy. This kind of bland and meaningless existence has been captured by those who imagine dystopian futures such as Aldous Huxley in his famous book *Brave New World*. In this futuristic dystopia people live endlessly comfortable lives, have medication for any sign of discontent, and mostly have very little pain or emotional discomfort with which to contend. What is most ironic about these endlessly happy visions of the future is that they *are* dystopian – the notion of endless happiness can start to feel a little scary and sickening. It is not unlike the way in which the pleasure of chocolate can quickly be turned into a form of torture if we are made to eat it continuously. Endless pleasure quickly becomes very painful. For true well-being or eudemonia we needs contrasts – pain makes pleasure all the more pleasurable and sadness gives meaning and context to happiness. Following this vein of thinking my colleagues and I have been recently spending quite a bit of time focusing on the benefits of pain.[12] Pain and sadness are important human experiences that are not simply bad and unwanted, but can have positive outcomes and may even be necessary for our very capacity to experience pleasure and happiness.

Loving happiness is not really the main problem here at all. Rather, it is when our love of happiness turns into a dislike of sadness that we experience the kinds of issues that I have described. Of course, happiness (or positive emotional experiences) are only one half of the emotional spectrum. As humans we have evolved the capacity for a range of negative emotions ranging from fear and anger to stress and sadness. These emotions are functionally important – they tell us something about how we are interacting with our environment, whether those interactions are successful, whether we need to avoid certain interactions in the future, or whether there is danger ahead. Indeed we would not live very long lives without the innate capacity for pain and sadness. One only has to look at cases of those with the congenital inability to experience pain to see how important this capacity is for a long and healthy life. Along these lines some have even ventured to suggest that feelings of depression are functional, and lead to more risk avoidant behaviour in social relations, reducing the prospects of outright social rejection by others.[13]

So can you love happiness and still be happy? I would certainly maintain that you can. But you cannot expect to be able to feel happy, you cannot try to feel happy, and you cannot capture or own your happiness. Think for a moment of what it takes to love your partner, your children or your friends. In each of these cases the critical component of love is the ability to set the other free. Love itself breeds the risk of loss, and perhaps is only as powerful as the threat of that loss. Trying to own or control others is rarely considered an expression of true love. If you love happiness, then perhaps the best advice is to set it free. Be glad when it enters your life, but don't feel disappointed and hurt when it leaves again. Letting it go may be the best way to ensure that it comes back to you again in the future.

Endnotes

1   I. B. Mauss, M. Tamir, C. L. Anderson & N. S. Savino, 'Can seeking happiness make people unhappy? Paradoxical effects of valuing happiness', *Emotion*, vol. 11, 2011, pp. 807–15.

2   For a review see A. M. Grant & B. Schwartz, 'Too much of a good thing: the challenge and opportunity of the inverted U', *Perspectives on Psychological Science*, vol. 6, no. 1, 2011, pp. 61–76.

3   G. V. Bodenhausen, G. P. Kramer & K. Süsser, 'Happiness and stereotypic thinking in social judgment', *Journal of Personality and Social Psychology*, vol. 66, no. 4, 1994, pp. 621–32.

4   R. Ackermann & R. J. DeRubeis, 'Is depressive realism real?', *Clinical Psychology Review*, vol. 11, no. 5, 1991, pp. 565–84.

5   B. Ehrenreich, *Smile or Die: How Positive Thinking Fooled America and the World*, Granta Publications, London, 2009.

6   J. C. Wakefield & M. First, 'Clarifying the distinction between disorder and non-disorder: Confronting the overdiagnosis ("false positives") problem in *DSM–V*', in K. A. Phillips, M. B. First & H. A. Pincus (eds), *Advancing* DSM: *Dilemmas in Psychiatric Diagnosis*, American Psychiatric Press, Washington DC, 2003, pp. 23–56.

7   E. G. Wilson, *Against Happiness: In Praise of Melancholy*, Sarah Crighton Books, New York, 2008.

8   J. R. Averill, 'Studies on anger and aggression: Implications for theories of emotion', *American Psychologist*, vol. 38, 1983, pp. 1145–60; A. H. Fischer & A. S. R. Manstead, 'Social functions of emotion' in M. Lewis, J. M. Haviland-Jones & L. Feldman Barrett (eds), *Handbook of Emotions*, Guilford, New York, 3rd ed, 2008, pp. 456–70.

9   S. C. Hayes, K. Strosahl & K. G. Wilson, *Acceptance and Commitment Therapy: Understanding and Treating Human Suffering*, Guilford Press, New York, 1999.

10 B. Bastian, P. Kuppens, K. De Roover & E. Diener, 'Is valuing positive emotion associated with life satisfaction?', *Emotion*, vol. 14, no. 4, August 2014, pp. 639–45.

11 B. Bastian, P. Kuppens, M. J. Hornsey, J. Park, P. Koval & Y. Uchida, 'Feeling bad about being sad: The role of social expectancies in amplifying negative mood', *Emotion*, vol. 12, 2012, pp. 69–80.

12 B. Bastian, J. Jetten, M. J. Hornsey & S. Leknes, 'The positive consequences of pain: A biopsychosocial approach', *Personality and Social Psychology Review*, vol. 18, no. 3, 2014, pp. 256–79.

13 N. B. Allen & P. B. Badcock, 'The social risk hypothesis of depressed mood: evolutionary, psychosocial, and neurobiological perspectives', *Psychological Bulletin*, vol. 129, no. 6, 2003, pp. 887–913.

ANGER AND COURAGE: THE DAUGHTERS OF HOPE

Richard Hamilton

> *'Hope has two beautiful daughters; their names are Anger and Courage. Anger at the way things are, and Courage to see that they do not remain as they are.'*

St Augustine of Hippo

The world is a pretty miserable place, all told. Most people live in squalid conditions, struggling to survive in the face of starvation, disease or military strife. Some enjoy a modicum of comfort (largely at the expense of the majority) yet the endless accumulation of trinkets brings little satisfaction. As the recent global financial crisis has shown, our relatively high living standards are precarious and easily undermined by a panic among the cocaine-addled gamblers on the stock exchange. Looming over all of us is an ecological catastrophe, which our dysfunctional political institutions lack the will or the wherewithal to tackle. A range of responses is open to us, from resignation to wishful thinking. In what follows, I will consider which response is the most appropriate and will suggest that happiness involves the right kind of hope, which in turn relies upon the proper combination of anger and courage.

Utopians have had a chequered history in political thought. Conservatives sneer at them for failing to recognise the darker side of human nature which will inevitably frustrate any attempt to wrest power from rich, old white men.[1] Even those on the left, who should presumably sympathise with the craving for a better world, have tended to share Engels' preference for pragmatic realpolitik over utopian dreaming.[2] More than twenty years after the demise of 'actually existing socialism' and the catastrophe that has been market triumphalism, it is unclear what we have gained from the left's embrace of pragmatism, other than rampant inequality and endless war.

Psychology is a different case. Particularly in its popular varieties, utopianism is the order of the day. Every time we open a newspaper or click on a link, we find ourselves enjoined to embrace positive thinking and invite wealth, love and professional success into our lives. While positive thinking in small doses might be merely irritating, there is a dark side to all of this. On the one hand, it can lead us to ignore the stark realities of social and economic inequality to a point at which our ignorance verges on delusional. Real wages and the standard of living have plummeted in the United States and other Western nations from the 1970s onwards and with them social mobility.[3] Yet surveys consistently show an increase in those who agree with statements about America being a land of opportunity, paradoxically greatest among those least likely to experience significant social mobility.[4] On the other, the belief in the power of positive thinking can, among the more fortunate, undermine compassion towards the unlucky. If a positive mental attitude and sufficient derring-do is all that is needed to beat cancer or poverty, why should we feel sorry for those who succumb to either?

Much of this reflects our peculiar vulnerability to self-deception. It is a well-established fact that those who are successful are much more likely to attribute their good fortune to personal factors than they are to social context or sheer dumb luck.[5] Even more troubling is the ubiquity of victim blaming. From the late 1970s onwards, Melvin Lerner has amassed data demonstrating the existence of a cognitive bias which he refers to as the 'Just World Hypothesis'. This 'hypothesis', when spelt out, is so absurd that no rational person could seriously hold it: the world is fundamentally just and the distribution of reward and punishment is determined by desert. Lerner specifies the desert assumption as follows:

> A Person 'P' deserves outcome 'X' if P has met the appropriate preconditions for obtaining X. [...] If P does not get X, or receives something of less value than X, then P has not received all he or she deserves. Of course, the outcomes in question can be negative rather than positive. P has met the appropriate preconditions to avoid the undesirable Y.[6]

This heuristic enables us to reconcile the troubling facts of injustice with our desire that the world make sense. Lerner suggests that we resort to the 'Just World Hypothesis' in situations where we are unable to help the victims of misfortune. We feel less discomfort if we can convince ourselves that the victim deserved their fate. Lerner's most troubling empirical research concerns a widespread propensity to blame victims of sexual violence. He was struck by the fact that those whom one would expect to be most sympathetic, namely other women, were often harshest in their judgements about the victims' culpability.[7] One plausible explanation for this phenomenon is that if the assault can be interpreted as the result of some poor choice the victim made, rather than sheer misfortune, this provides the onlooker with reassurance: since she would not make such choices, she is unlikely to be victimised.

The Just World bias also helps to explain much contemporary politics, particularly in the USA where populist right-wing forces such as the Tea Party have been able to divert attention away from the true causes of the recession, redirecting them towards immigrants, those on welfare and people of colour. If one comes to believe that others are poor because of personal moral failings rather than through structural inequalities over which we have little control, this can help to explain an otherwise inexplicable world. However, consider for a moment the much more plausible possibility that the world, rather than being organised along rational and just lines, is a fundamentally unjust place. Accidents of birth have significantly more bearing on one's life chances than any other factor and misfortune is a built-in feature of the human condition.

What would be the appropriate response in such a situation? The Ancient Greeks had an answer. Their drama emphasised that fate was cruel and tragedy unavoidable. One cannot avoid misfortune and one's only choice in its face was how valiantly one dealt with it. This way of thinking reaches its apogee in Stoicism, the greatest intellectual movement of the Hellenistic period. Through its influence on the Roman Empire and Early Christian Thought, Stoicism has become a feature of the

European intellectual landscape. We recognise it in our ordinary expression 'stoical', although this common understanding differs radically from its traditional meaning.

At first blush, it is hard to see what Stoicism may have to teach us about happiness. We tend to see a stoic as someone who is grimly unemotional. The Stoics themselves, however, did not dispute the contention of their contemporaries that happiness was the goal of human life; they differed only on the means to achieve it. For the Stoics, true happiness is only possible when we are able to still disruptive emotions which prevent us from seeing reality as it truly is. In other words, we must embrace what Freud many centuries later referred to as 'the reality principle'.[8] To achieve this, the Stoics thought, we must foster a range of intellectual and moral virtues, a process that involves rigorous training. We achieve happiness circuitously, since we achieve it only if we become virtuous.

To modern ears this may sound odd. We tend not to think of happiness as something for which we need to be trained and the connection between virtue and happiness appears implausible. This highlights a radical distinction between Hellenistic and modern moral psychology. For all their differences, the various Hellenistic philosophical schools tended to be united in seeing happiness not as an occurrent psychological state, but as a property of an entire life. Even stranger to modern ears is the idea that happiness is an objective and not a subjective matter: that one can in fact be deeply mistaken about it. Yet, when we reflect upon it at a deeper level, both of these truths become clearer. A parent whose deepest wish is that his children live a happy life probably does not envisage such a life for them as one where every wish is granted. The capacity for regret (which all but psychopaths and capitalists possess) involves a recognition that not all of our desires are worth pursuing and that we may often be misled about the worthiness of their objects.

A seemingly arcane debate in Hellenistic ethics has tremendous relevance here. This debate turns on the so-called 'sufficiency thesis' and the role of external goods in happiness. The 'sufficiency thesis', which the Stoics associated with Socrates, is the claim that virtue is not merely necessary for happiness – most Greek thinkers agreed that it was – but that it was also sufficient. The question of external goods concerned whether one needs to acquire any of the goods which conventional opinion associates with happiness, such as material wealth and social status. The worry about external goods tallies with recent discussions of 'affluenza'. It does not appear that the accumulation of wealth has much bearing on well-being. Indeed, the opposite appears to be the case. Once we have enough money to provide security, financial incentives become demotivating. This makes logical sense: there is no reason to suppose that possessing a billion dollars makes one a thousand times happier than possessing a million, nor owning two yachts makes one twice as happy as owning one.

Many Hellenistic philosophers drew the rather extreme conclusion that external goods were entirely irrelevant to happiness. Epicurus, for instance, allegedly claimed that the sage could find happiness in any situation even (notoriously) while being tortured on the rack.[9] Contrary to the stereotype of the Epicurean, his followers trained themselves to moderate their tastes so as to avoid the diminishing pleasure caused by overindulgence. As attractive as such disdain for material wealth and conventional success may seem from the vantage point of our celebrity-obsessed consumerist culture, it does raise a significant issue.

If virtue is sufficient for happiness, then what incentive do we have for opposing gross inequality or political oppression? The sage could surely find the internal resources to be happy even in a dictatorship. It is a notable feature of the Stoic movement that its two most significant thinkers, Marcus Aurelius and Epictetus, represented the polar opposites of Roman society. Marcus Aurelius was one of the greatest emperors, while Epictetus was a freed slave.

The issue of slavery is a particularly pointed one. Julia Annas, a modern admirer of the Stoics, gives considerable attention to this topic. The issue which troubles her is that the Stoics, who are clearly impeccable in so many other respects, appear to have a blind spot when it comes to slavery. Although some Roman Stoics advance arguments in favour of respecting the slave's dignity and capacity for virtue – and none go to Aristotle's lengths in constructing a specious justification of the institution – they seem unable to envisage a world that does not rely upon it. Even Aurelius, while emperor, never legislated to modify the institution or ameliorate the condition of slaves. Annas compares the Greeks' situation with that of nineteenth-century Britons, for whom slavery was also a central feature of the socio-economic system, who yet were able to achieve abolition.

Lest we become too complacent, Annas draws a parallel between the position of the Roman Stoics and our own with regards to the hyper-exploitation of the developing world.

> We in developed countries recognize that globaliza-
> tion, especially in recent forms, has produced patterns

of dominance and exploitation which now benefit us in ways that cannot ethically be defended. What, however, can individual efforts do to improve such a large scale situation? Our position is rather like that of the Roman Stoic convinced of the ethical untenability of slavery, but unable individually to do anything effective or to make any impact on the institution. Future generations will think of us in much the same way we think of the Roman Stoics, as doing the right thing (some of us) but as having a fundamentally compromised virtue.[10]

Annas suggests that this may be the best we can do. We will always be imperfectly virtuous and the properly Stoic course of action is to attend to those aspects of our life that we can affect, for instance our personal relationships, rather than engaging in grandiose projects of resistance that may be more about vanity than virtue.

Herein lies the greatest danger of Stoicism as an ethical view, a tendency towards quietism in the face of intolerable injustice. Perhaps the point at which Stoicism has nothing useful to say about an ethical issue is the point at which ethics must become political philosophy. In other words, it is the point at which we reach the limits of individual action and must deliberate and act collectively about the kind of society we want. The fact is that slavery eventually disappeared from the Ancient Worlds, largely as a result of the social and moral revolution represented by early Christianity, an inspiration to which nineteenth-century abolitionists directly appealed. It was a movement consciously driven by the hope of a better world, albeit one beyond this mortal coil. The moral and ecological challenges of our time demand a response of a similar scale. The question facing us is what sort of spirit should animate such a movement?

One of Marx's most famous adages refers to religion as the 'opiate of the masses' yet the quotation is seldom given in full. Here it is:

> Religious suffering is, at one and the same time, the expression of real suffering and a protest against real suffering. Religion is the sigh of the oppressed creature, the heart of a heartless world, and the soul of soulless conditions. It is the opium of the people.[11]

Given the all-too-frequent alliances between religious hierarchies and other institutionalised forces of oppression, it is understandable that political progressives have tended to emphasise the stultifying effects of religion, offering us 'pie in the sky' in return for accepting starvation wages in the here and now. Nevertheless, it is hard to ignore the influence of religious sentiment in every progressive movement from the American Civil Rights movement through to contemporary ecological activism. Marx's quotation recognises this ambivalence.

One Marxian thinker who has explored the connection between religious sentiment and movements that aspire to change the world of the here and now, rather than waiting for some messianic future is Ernst Bloch. In his magnum opus, *The Principle of Hope* (1954), Bloch explores the utopian impulse as it has figured in political, religious and artistic thought. He locates this utopian spirit in the universal human propensity for daydreaming, for imagining reality to be other than it actually is. He notes that some forms of daydreaming are merely escapist and avoid the hard work involved in building real alternatives.

Yet it is hard to imagine any progressive movement which does not embody a spirit of utopianism, if we understand it in Bloch's sense as the insistence that 'the not-yet-become' is more real than the past and present. Leaving aside the metaphysical difficulties to which this view gives rise, let us counterpose it to its alternative a dull-headed empiricism in which the 'traditions of dead generations weighs like a nightmare on the brains of the living'.[12]

In a masterly study of conservative rhetoric Albert O. Hirschmann outlines three theses that characterise reactionary thought. They are

> the *perversity thesis*, or the thesis of perverse effect, the *futility thesis*, and the *jeopardy thesis*. According to the *perversity thesis*, any purposive action to improve some feature of the social, political or economic order only serves to exacerbate the conditions one wishes to remedy. The *futility thesis* holds that attempts at social transformation will be unavailing, that they will simply 'fail to make a dent'. Finally, the *jeopardy thesis* argues that the cost of the proposed change or reform is too high as it endangers some previous, precious accomplishment.[13]

What characterises conservatism (which frequently goes under the name of realism or pragmatism) is an extreme aversion to risk. Actually, to be more precise, it would be better to say that it is averse to certain kinds of risks, since conservatives generally have no problem with the risks involved in continuing to tolerate gross inequality or environmental degradation.

Conservatives are like petulant children who spend their time knocking down others' sandcastles rather than building their own. Genuine progressive thought, by contrast, embraces risk, recognising that, as Whitehead wrote, 'the great advances of Civilisation are processes which all but wreck the societies in which they occur'[14]. Some institutions are simply not worth preserving. The abolition of slavery would have never occurred had the abolitionists been overcome by fear of change. Real change requires us to think the unthinkable. In order to do so, we must, as Bloch suggests, learn how to hope. We do this through exercising our imagination by exposing it to art, to the religious impulse and to the best forms of philosophical thinking.

Clearly, not all forms of hope are equally valid, just as not all forms of risk aversion are bad. We need to distinguish between that hope which is little more than wishful thinking – the sort peddled by positive-thinking gurus – and the sort of hope which is prepared to stare reality starkly in the face and yet still be prepared to imagine a better world. It goes without saying that such hope requires courage. It also, as the quotation from Augustine with which we opened indicates, comes accompanied with a degree of anger that the world is not as it should be.

Anger represents a uniquely problematic case for rationalist philosophy. It seems to be the polar opposite of the calm acceptance of how things are. Seneca famously counselled against anger, arguing that it always arose from an infantile frustration with the conflict between our desires and the facts. This Stoic position has much merit. We are familiar with the destructive consequences of rage, no matter how righteous its inspiration. Yet, to fail to be angry at injustice indicates a failure of compassion. As Aristotle suggests, someone who 'endures beings insulted and...puts up with insults to one's friends' is morally defective.[15]

In the context of a discussion of happiness this then is the paradox: rationality seems to demand both the angry rejection of actually existing reality and calm acceptance of the facts, yet how is such a conflicted set of attitudes compatible with happiness? Calm acceptance can quickly degenerate into either despair or wishful thinking, but anger brings costs of its own.

In her masterly analysis of the 'burdened virtues' associated with political resistance, Lisa Teesman offers an insightful discussion of political anger. She locates this in the context of Aristotle's Doctrine of the Mean, which in her interpretation implies that in certain circumstances even rage might be the appropriate response. However, as she notes:

> [i]f tremendous anger is ultimately unhealthy or corrosive for its bearer, then the political resister with an angry disposition displays an example of what I have been calling a burdened virtue: a morally praiseworthy trait that is at the same time bad for its bearer, disconnected from its bearer's well-being. The resister to oppression faces a dilemma that challenges or burdens the virtues [...] if one chooses to be angry only in a measured way, then one must endure degradation of oneself or others on behalf of whom one acts, but if

one chooses to develop a fully angered/enraged disposition in response to the vast injustice one is fighting, then the anger can become consuming.[16]

One might point to those rare examples (Ghandi or Nelson Mandela perhaps) who somehow seem to transcend this dilemma – resisting oppression without anger – but the point is surely that they are rare. It is the hallmark of systematically oppressive societies that it is virtually impossible for the nonheroic to resist or endure them without substantial cost to their own well-being, and in the case of both Ghandi and Mandela their political success came at substantial personal cost. Our task then is to create communities that have no need for heroes; communities in which ordinarily decent individuals can flourish. In order to create them, we require the peculiar combination of courage and anger that is the necessary corollary of hope. Perhaps then we might dream of happiness.

Endnotes

1   J. Kekes, *Against Liberalism*, Cornell University Press, New York, 1999; *Straw Dogs: Thoughts on Humans and Other Animals*, Granta, London, 2007.

2   F. Engels, *Socialism: Utopian and Scientific*, Pathfinder Press, New York, 2008.

3   As meticulously detailed in T. Piketty, *Capital in the Twenty-First Century*, Bellknap Press, Cambridge, 2014.

4   The Pew Charitable Trusts, *Pursuing the American Dream: Economic Mobility Across Generations*, viewed 30 September 2014, http://www.pewtrusts.org/en/research-and-analysis/reports/0001/01/01/pursuing-the-american-dream.

5   J. Doris, *Lack of Character: Personality and Moral Behavior*, Cambridge University Press, Cambridge, 2002, p. 93.

6   M. J. Lerner, *Belief In A Just World: A Fundamental Delusion*, Springer Science and Business Media, New York, 1980, p. 11.

7   M. Lerner & L. Montada (eds.), *Responses to Victimization and Belief in a Just World*, Springer, New York, 1998.

8   S. Freud, *Civilization and its Discontents (Complete Psychological Works of Sigmund Freud)*, WH Norton, New York & London, 2010.

9   J. Annas, *The Morality of Happiness*, Oxford University Press, Oxford, 1998, p. 349.

10   J. Annas *Intelligent Virtue*, Oxford University Press, Oxford, 2011, p. 64.

11   K. Marx, *Contribution to a Critique of Hegel's Philosophy of Right*, 1843, Marxist Internet Archive, viewed 29 September 2014, http://marxists. org/archive/marx/works/1843/critique-hpr/intro.htm.

12   K. Marx, *The 18th Brumaire of Louis Bonaparte*, 1852, Marxist Internet Archive, viewed 29 September 2014, https://www.marxists.org/ archive/marx/works/1852/18th-brumaire/.

13   A. O. Hirschmann, *The Rhetoric of Reaction: Perversity, Futility, Jeopardy*, The Bellknap Press of Harvard University Press, Cambridge MA & London, 1991, p. 6.

14   A. N. Whitehead, *Symbolism*, New York Capricorn (reprint ed.), 1959, p. 88, quoted in Hirschman op. cit. p. 3.

15   Aristotle, *Nicomachean Ethics* (1126a7-8).

16   L. Teesman. *Burdened Virtues: Virtue Ethics For Liberatory Struggles*, Oxford University Press, Oxford, 2005, pp. 124–5.

BLISSED OUT – ON HEDONOPHOBIA

Steven Connor

Difficulty with Pleasure

We have difficulty with pleasure, which makes it hard for us to know or tell the truth about much of what we do and why we do it. Part of our difficulty with pleasure comes from the fact of the professionalisation of it. When Montaigne withdrew from the world to devote himself to contemplation of the world and of himself, it is plain that this was no monkish renunciation, but rather a determination to devote himself unswervingly to the highest, most sustained and sustaining pleasure he could imagine. Montaigne was able to do this because he was possessed of plenty of money and therefore of leisure. If he had instead been offered the Chair of Contemplation Studies at the University of Louvain, it is a pretty sure thing that the work he produced would have been considerably less pleasurable, both for him and us – less various, less amused and amusing, less joyous – than the essays he produced in his long and vigorous retirement from the world. It is an awkward thing to be professionally committed to the study of forms of pleasure, as professors – using the word in the broadest sense – of art, literature and music might reasonably be thought to be. Such persons, along with critics, curators and other mediators of the pleasurable arts, tend to want to emphasise the earnestness and utility of what they do. The point of any theory of art produced under professional circumstances, or the kinds of professional circumstances that operate in our kind of society, is overwhelmingly likely to be that it emphasises the things other than 'mere' pleasure that art may be thought to offer – typically, nowadays, the value of analytic instruction, laying bare the operations or effects of wickedness (in the form of various sorts of abstract systems of power, capitalism, colonialism, etc) or of encouraging resistance to various unpalatable forms of social and political arrangement. Art is overwhelmingly construed as helping us to see, or to feel good things, and, if we take pleasure in such things, it is the accessory or subordinate pleasure of a duty well-performed.

We are, in fact, today beset by the ravening beast of earnestness. The least bad thing about this is that it is dull and enervating. The worst thing about it is that it provides so many opportunities for bullying and coercion. The demotion of pleasure allows those who put themselves on the side of duty and requirement – and this is to say, those who are appointed or take themselves to be appointed professionally or administratively to do so – to insist that we sign up to their patterns of duty and requirement.

But it is not just a matter of the casual routinisation of pleasure. A more fundamental problem may be its systematic availability. We have become a society devoted to play and entertainment. I do not mean this in the kind of blimpish sense that might have been employed by any killjoy or Savonarola at almost any point in history, against any particular group, whether it be concupiscent clergy or the rakish aristocracy or even the feckless working class crowding into the cinemas in the 1950s, which so disquieted left-liberal critics of a Leavisite or Adornian stamp. What seems to be new is that we have indeed become for the first time a society that is organised not around work and production but around play and entertainment. Adorno was right to see play and leisure as inseparable from labour, since our economies are dedicated to and sternly orientated around the production of pleasure. It is not so much that we have moved from a production- to a consumption-based economy as that what we primarily produce is play, pleasure and entertainment. Pleasure and leisure used to be marginal – variously snatched, harboured and rescued from a background of routine work. Now the production and distribution of pleasure-surplus has become economically structural. The fact that the production of pleasure is such grindingly hard graft, and that the consumption of pleasure something like an economic responsibility, is another reason for our difficulty with pleasure.

Hence the phenomenon of compulsive pleasure or, as we know it more familiarly, addiction. In this sense, we might perhaps take addiction to be the most representative hedonopathic form. Addiction literally means an assignment, or giving over; an addict, is one who is *addictus*, from *ad* and *dicere*, made over, appointed. The earliest uses of the word in English suggest a voluntary giving over of oneself – 'the state or condition of being dedicated or devoted to a thing, esp. an activity or occupation', as *OED* definition 1a of the word addiction has it. The fact that the earliest example of the word in English is modified by the word 'overmuch' suggests that it does not automatically have that meaning of excessive devotion, though it seems quickly to have acquired it.

Addiction stands to pleasure as obsession does to devotion. If every era has its signature illness – hysteria for the late nineteenth century, multiple personality disorder for the

1950s – then the representative malady of our time may well be obsessive-compulsive disorder. Like obsession, addiction provides a kind of anchor amidst a world otherwise experienced as dizzying, but tediously unvarying distraction. Addiction may be regarded as a kind of extreme brand loyalty. An addictive relation to a pleasure can also come about when the pleasure moves from being marginal to being structural, when we start to need to count on pleasure, and the uncertainty of the pleasure becomes a source of extreme anxiety. Pleasure turns oddly on the hinge between freedom and slavery. When my pleasures are for me, they remain nonaddictive. When I become dependent on my pleasures, they are no longer me, I am for them. They become hard labour, that to which I have been assigned or made over.

So, on the one hand, we have a world in which the production of pleasure is seemingly more central than ever before and, on the other, a world in which we seem only to have the most parched language for the discussion or acknowledgement of pleasure.

Thinking Pleasure

It would be easy to represent this situation in terms of the loss of spontaneity. But pleasure is rarely spontaneous, and when it is it may be in proportion ephemeral and unsustaining. Pleasure in fact has the reputation of being the ephemeral itself, and we are consequentially often enjoined, by Stoics, Christians and other wet-blanket otherworldians of every denomination to turn aside from the impermanence of pleasure to the lasting virtues of truth and duty. And yet pleasure must also be taken, which is to say, taken account of. Dickens captures this very well in *Martin Chuzzlewit*, in a scene in which the character Tom Pinch sits in a bar in Salisbury:

> All the farmers being by this time jogging homewards, there was nobody in the sanded parlour of the tavern where he had left the horse; so he had his little table drawn out close before the fire, and fell to work upon a well-cooked steak and smoking hot potatoes, with a strong appreciation of their excellence, and a very keen sense of enjoyment. Beside him, too, there stood a jug of most stupendous Wiltshire beer; and the effect of the whole was so transcendent, that he was obliged every now and then to lay down his knife and fork, rub his hands, and think about it.[1]

That this is a comic moment might aptly remind us of Freud's complex negotiations with the economies of laughter. The essence of the Freudian theory of the comic, which significantly is not focused on the unbound energies of spontaneous hilarity, but on the geared machinations of the joke, is that it involves the differential investment of quantities of psychic labour, in order to manufacture a tension that can be profitably released as laughter. This is a local application of the general economic principle in Freud that there is no pleasure – or at least no pleasure as sweet – without the overcoming or outwitting of obstacles.

Pleasure is never simple – it is always in fact duplicitous (at least). In this it does not resemble pain, which is immediate, self-announcing and self-interpreting. Pain can be diffuse, and difficult to describe, but there is rarely any doubt that it is there. Perhaps this is why pain has so often been thought of as the guarantee of the real. Pleasure, and the desire for it seem, by contrast, much less certain or self-evident, and much more intrinsically difficult simply to experience. You seem to have, like Tom Pinch, to give it some thought.

Whereas pain saturates and yet also abolishes time, pleasure is intimately intermingled with temporal experience, from which it borrows. The anticipation of pleasure, even if it is in the negative form of the retreat of pain, gives tone, texture and extension to time. It is hard to think of a pleasure that does not involve or require some kind of protention or retrospection. So, where pain is absolute, pleasure is relative. Pleasure can never be wholly *en-soi*, or in itself, it must always be in part *pour-soi*, for itself, which is to say, it must involve some minimal form of reflexivity. It is for this reason that it seems to make sense to say that one might suddenly become aware that something is, or was pleasurable, but it does not seem easy to conceive how one might be in pain without realising it. There are two contrary ways of thinking of this. First of all, one might say that pleasure is never fully aware of itself, that it is not until it is represented in some way that it can be recognised as pleasure. But I would prefer to say that pleasure is always compound in form, that is, it always involves some kind of estimation or taking stock. This implies that pain or difficulty are not the opposites of pleasure, but part of its repertoire.

One of the principal forms of pleasure's reflexivity is the subjecting of it to metric and quantification. The conjoining of work, pleasure and number is nowhere better evidenced than in the development of modern sport. Before the massive and ramified codification of sports that took place in the later nineteenth century, almost exclusively in England, not insignificantly the most advanced industrial nation in the world, little account was taken of measurement or scoring in sport. A medieval football match between two villages, which might last all day and lead to many broken heads and limbs, ended when one team scored. There was no opportunity to go for an equaliser, no change of ends, no best-of-three or penalty shoot-out. Victory was absolute, crushing and final. Though we may try to pretend that we have lost something vivid and precious in the replacement of the all-or-nothing excess of carnival sports by rules and scoring systems, in fact this is part of a process of redistributing the capital of pleasure.

Taking Stock of Pleasure

We have convinced ourselves, especially the we that is presupposed and presumed upon among a gathering of nonmathematical persons, that, whatever else it may do, the mathematisation of the world must pose a threat to our humanity and freedom. 'I am not a number' roared the Patrick McGoohan character at the beginning of each episode of the 1960s cult series *The Prisoner*, 'I am a free man'. If there is one binding article of faith among those in the humanities, and there are of course many, it is that there is a deep and dangerous antagonism between the realm of number and the realm of words and images. The realm of the qualitative must be secured against the deadening incursions of the quantitative. The presence or prominence of number is the great discriminator between the sciences and the humanities. The more the realm of number expands, we fear, and thereby also reassure ourselves, the more the realm of the human diminishes. We know it, we are sure of it, we have no need to think about it anymore, indeed we cannot waste or risk time thinking about it, lest we cease to be able to think with it.

In his *Art of Discovery* of 1685, Leibniz looked forward to the day when calculation might take the place of disputation:

> The only way to rectify our reasonings is to make them as tangible as those of the Mathematicians, so that we can find our error at a glance, and when there are disputes among persons, we can simply say: Let us calculate [*calculemus*], without further ado, to see who is right.[2]

Nevertheless, a defining strain preparing for the contemporary allergy to number in the humanities is the Romantic protest against the powerful efforts to put social and political reasoning on a firm basis by employing calculative reason, especially in the philosophical form of utilitarianism. A central figure in that history is Charles Dickens, whose critique of utilitarianism is embodied in the figure of Thomas Gradgrind in *Hard Times*, who is introduced to us as:

> A man of realities. A man of facts and calculations. A man who proceeds upon the principle that two and two are four, and nothing over, and who is not to be talked into allowing for anything over... With a rule and a pair of scales, and the multiplication table always in his pocket, sir, ready to weigh and measure any parcel of human nature, and tell you exactly what

it comes to. It is a mere question of figures, a case of simple arithmetic.[3]

Jeremy Bentham was not the first, but was certainly the most systematic and influential exponent of utilitarian philosophy; that is, the philosophy that insists that the value of anything is to be defined wholly and without residue in terms of its utility, or its tendency to produce 'benefit, advantage, pleasure, good, or happiness'.[4] I am one of his sect. I stand before you an unrepentant utilitarian, if also, I hope, a more versatile one than Thomas Gradgrind. Quantity and measurement are at the heart of utility, since the utility of an action or idea arises when 'the tendency it has to augment the happiness of the community is greater than any which it has to diminish it'.[5] Bentham did in all earnestness, and to the quick derision of many, propose what he called a 'felicific calculus' that would allow one to calculate the exact quantity of pleasures and pains. Since Bentham's single governing moral principle was the production of pleasure and the reduction of pain for the greatest number, such an effort at quantification was unavoidable.

The felicific calculus is set out in chapter four of his *Introduction to the Principles of Morals and Legislation* (1789), which is entitled 'Value of a Lot of Pleasure or Pain, How to Be Measured'. There he distinguished seven different dimensions of the pleasures or unpleasures that might be produced by a given action. These dimensions were: 1) the intensity of the pleasure or pain; 2) its likely duration; 3) its certainty or uncertainty; 4) its propinquity or remoteness; 5) its fecundity, by which Bentham means 'the chance it has of being followed by sensations of the same kind'; 6) its purity, that is 'or the chance it has of not being followed by sensations of the opposite kind'; and, finally, 7), its extent, that is, the number of persons whom it may affect.[6] Bentham even produced a mnemonic jingle to help his students keep this algorithm in mind:

> *Intense, long, certain, speedy, fruitful, pure –*
> Such marks in *pleasures* and in *pains* endure.
> Such pleasures seek if *private* be thy end:
> If it be *public,* wide let them *extend.*
> Such *pains* avoid, whichever be thy view:
> If pains *must* come, let them *extend* to few.[7]

Moral reflection is thereby reduced – or maybe raised – to mathematical reasoning. The usual, and right, thing to say about the hedonic calculus is that it is impossible to do the sums. The usual, but erroneous thing to say about why this is is that pleasure and number are inimical, or that pleasure is unquantifiable. It is true that one of the real problems with Bentham's calculus is that it presupposes some common measure or single currency, which would allow one in principle to add and subtract between these different qualities. Bentham was frank in his acknowledgement that the closest approximation we have to this common measure is money. It is perhaps for this reason that utilitarian philosophers have sometimes adopted the terms hedons and dolours for the units of felicific currency. Later in the book, in the course of a discussion of the proportioning of offences and punishments, Bentham deals with the objection that 'passion does not calculate', to which his simple and straightforward response is that it is not true. The Benthamite reply to the objection that we cannot quantify pleasure is that we so manifestly and continuously do.

Men calculate, some with less exactness, indeed, some with more: but all men calculate. I would not say, that even a madman does not calculate. Passion calculates, more or less, in every man: "in different men, according to the warmth or coolness of their dispositions: according to the firmness or irritability of their minds: according to the nature of the motives by which they are acted upon". [8]

The real problem with the felicific calculus is not that it enforces calculation where none is possible, but that there are so many ways of doing the calculations. The problem is not that the felicific calculus is too rigid and inapplicable to the circumstances of pleasure, but, as Wesley C. Mitchell observed many years ago, that it is too obliging to them.[9] But this does not diminish the fact that pleasure and measure are in fact tightly intertwined. Far from being the adversary of number, pleasure is, in some ways, its apotheosis.

Working with Pleasure

One of the great sources of pain attaching to the question of pleasure is that we persist in thinking of pleasure as the inverse of work. The harder we work, the less pleasure we have, the less work we do, the more pleasure we will have. We should be cautious and sceptical whenever we find ourselves reasoning on the basis that anything is the opposite of anything else, but particularly when it comes to pleasure. Since pleasure is the motive principle of everything we do, it finds ways of insinuating itself into everything that seems inimical to it. When I was a student, I had a number of menial jobs in factories and the like, and, like many in such circumstances, I found the tedium of the work hugely depressing and fatiguing. Like many other student workers, the way I found to reduce these pains was not to shirk and skive, but to actually to throw myself into the work. I had, say, to spend all day on the de-burring machine, a little wheel that span and removed the rough snags on the side of the little rectangles of copper – ultimately to become printed circuits – that another machine had stamped out. I stood at the wheel with a pile of copper rectangles beside me that was almost my height, and my job was to de-burr them. It was easily possible to do four or five of these a minute, but it was very hard indeed to carry on doing four or five a minute for sixty minutes an hour and for seven hours a day. But, if I set myself the task of doing, say six or seven a minute, things changed. Simply varying the number of copper rectangles I managed to de-burr a minute somehow sweetened, or de-burred the task itself, just a little, but, given its soul-corroding monotony, a little was more than enough. And, of course, once I realised that I was getting better at the task, and was regularly achieving rates of six or seven a minute, I began to wonder whether I might not be able to do eight for, say, three or even four consecutive minutes. This required vigilance and planning. I needed to bring my performance under critical review, assessing the ways in which I picked up the copper oblongs, and even the order in which I did them. I laid wagers with myself, devised inducements and rewards for prolonged good performance.

By subjecting my performance to mechanical survey, and calculating outcomes and margins, I escaped the condition of mechanisation to which I was otherwise painfully delivered. At the same time I discovered a further source of pleasure in the reckoning itself. Even if I flagged and failed to reach my targets, even if the breakneck exhilaration of doing eight de-burrings a minute began to pall, I had at least the fact of the calculative perspective open to me. I had a critical relation to the work I was doing, a relation that, insofar as it was calculative, was in fact playful. I was not just calculating my pleasure, I was pleasing myself with my calculations.

All students and newcomers to circumstances in which not very exacting work must be done at a steady rate over a sustained period will sooner or later discover the pleasure of subjecting things to measure in order to go beyond it. And most of those tyros will also sooner or later be made forcibly aware that there is in fact a complicating calculation to be made. For I was going to be working in that factory for, at most, six weeks. The people I was working alongside had been in the job for years and much depended for them on their being able to remain in it for many further years. Most of them had found the optimum level of performance, that balanced out all the countervailing pressures and could be sustained, day in and day out, over long periods, even, if necessary lifelong. Though it might well be possible for them to match the blistering rate of production to which I aspired and which I was able intermittently to attain, I was like a quarter-miler setting the pace for a marathon, and it was not going to be possible for them to maintain that rate for the rest of their working lives. I had to be stopped, and, of course, I was. I was forced, by means of various blandishments and ethical humiliations, to ease off, and the work became again, as it had been at the beginning, slow-dripping torture. I had discovered that it was easier to work hard than to take it easy; indeed, that, under certain circumstances, ease was agony.

I became a socialist at that point and alas see no prospect of ever being able to unbecome one, though it was not until later that I realised the kind of socialist I was. I realised that what mattered was not the quality of life that was achieved and how the chances of it were distributed under a given social arrangement. Nor did it fundamentally matter that the people who did most of the work did not get most of the profit, important though that is. What mattered, for the Romantic Morrisian I became, well before ever reading any of the insipid works of William Morris, was not the profit that might be made from work, but the quality of the work that it was possible for people to do, or, at least the quality of the relation they had to their work. I was about to go to university to read English, and, whenever I was faced with reading my way through the *Faerie Queene* or the *Morte d'Arthur*, or, for that matter, the wearisome *News From Nowhere*, or learning a list of Old English verb inflections, I infallibly remembered my hours and days at the de-burring machine, and knew that I was in fact in Paradise, compared with not having work of such a kind to do. The real social divide then, and now, is not between people who are well and badly rewarded for the work they do, but between people who have work that they would do anyway for nothing, and people who would give anything not to have to do the work they do.

Much of our contemporary difficulty with pleasure comes from the fact that the relations between work and leisure have become so burred, blurred and uncertain. The response we should make is not to try to clarify or reassert the difference, but to enter into it. Because we are not as sensitive as we might be to the complex economies of work and play, our reasoning about the kinds of reasoning that are at work in our experiences and the pleasure that runs back and forth between them is fuzzy and impoverished.

Difficult Pleasure

Let me recall the itinerary I have followed. I have suggested first of all that we have various kinds of difficulty with pleasure, a difficulty that comes from the increasing abundance and availability of pleasures, forcing more and more people to internalise the limits and forms of regulation that scarcity had previously provided, as well as from the formalisation of pleasure that is a concomitant feature of the increasing abundance. This has produced a kind of Romantic blur and blunder about the ways in which pleasure is in fact intertwined with number and measure. Rather than attempting to rescue or purify pleasure from the difficulties it has got into, I have wanted to emphasise the paradoxical fact that pleasure is in fact entangled with, and even in some sense dependent upon, difficulty. If we have difficulty with pleasure, this is in part because we seem constituted to get such pleasure from difficulty. Rather than an idealising or essentialising quarantining of absolute pleasure, I recommend an enhanced utilitarianism, which cleaves to the principle that only utility can determine value, but recognises that there is no single unified currency, or principle of mensuration by which pleasures can be totted up, even as pleasure is, *ab initio*, and ever more irreducibly as time proceeds, utterly suffused by quantity and number. Leibniz was right, though not for reasons that he is likely to have approved. If we are to understand and account for our pleasure, then measure is indispensable. *Calculemus.*

Endnotes

1   C. Dickens, *Martin Chuzzlewit*, Margaret Cardwell (ed.), Oxford University Press, Oxford and New York, 1991, p. 66.
2   P. Wiener (ed.), *Leibniz: Selections*, Scribner, New York, 1951, p. 51.
3   C. Dickens, *Hard Times*, Paul Schlicke (ed.), Oxford University Press, Oxford, 2008, p. 8.
4   J. Bentham, *Introduction to the Principles of Morals and Legislation*, Clarendon Press, Oxford, 1907, p. 2.
5   ibid., p. 3.
6   ibid., p. 30.
7   ibid., p. 29.
8   ibid., pp. 187–8.
9   W. C. Mitchell, 'Bentham's Felicific Calculus', *Political Science Quarterly*, 1918, vol. 33, p. 180.

2

SOCIAL INTERROGATIONS

HAPPY HOUSEWIVES AND ANGRY FEMINISTS: THE MYTHS OF MODERN MOTHERHOOD

Camilla Nelson

You are standing in the checkout queue at Woolworths or Coles. You've managed to get the bulk of the family shopping and count yourself lucky, but there are drawbacks. Your 3-year-old is screaming because you wouldn't buy that brightly coloured plastic toy that was manufactured in an illegal sweatshop in the Philippines or Hong Kong. You crouch down to child height to explain in language that a 3-year-old can understand, only to find that your 18-month-old has swiped a caffeine-coated chocolate bar from the advertising display opposite the counter. You hand the drool-covered candy-bar to the store assistant and mouth the word 'Sorry', although what you really want to say is, 'What do you expect when child-attracting objects are displayed in grabbing distance from a pram or stroller?' Meanwhile, your 3-year-old has thrown himself full length on the supermarket floor, and is actually kicking his hands and feet. You are getting strange sideways glances from the customers around you, and now your 18-month-old is screaming too. You bring out your most potent weapon – the exit. Only you find that the shopping mall has been designed to delay your departure for as long as possible, in the expectation that some hapless consumer will make an additional unwanted purchase if delayed long enough.

Now if you were a 'good mother', according to the baby books, you would have planned your shopping trip around the children's sleep times, and therefore none of this should be occurring. Or else, you would have transformed the grocery shopping into a fun, educational opportunity – the grocery store, according to the parenting advice manual, is a real-world situation in which reading, maths and problem-solving are easily taught, along with nutrition, atomic science and astrophysics. At the very least, you should have brought along some broccoli poached in desalinated Perrier water as an allegedly attractive substitute for objects marketed by the multibillion-dollar toy and confectionary industry directed at children. You are an educated woman – in fact, you have three university degrees – and so you shouldn't really be surprised how often theory collapses in the face of gritty reality. But this doesn't stop you from feeling like the world's most terrible mother – indeed, there is some dark and fearful location at the back of your brain where you honestly believe the advice manual that stated, 'building wizard's castles out of lentils and mashed kumara is indispensable for your child's emotional well-being' might have been correct. You resolutely reject the call from your boss who keeps ringing on your mobile phone about an alleged crisis in the office that apparently cannot be solved without you. You are not such a dolt that you believe that you need to be remotely like the yummy mummies in the tabloids who have miraculously dropped 20 kilos within a millisecond of giving birth, but you feel as if you possess all the glamour of a hippopotamus in stretch pants as you drag your shopping trolley and screaming children down to the underground car park.

It seems as if three successive waves of feminism haven't resolved the chronic mismatch between the ideal of the 'good' and 'happy' mother and the realities of women's lives. Even if you consciously reject them, these ideas about what a mother *ought to be* and *ought to feel* are probably there from the minute you wake up until you go to bed at night.[1] Indeed, even in our age of increased gender equality it seems as if the culture loves nothing more than to dish out the myths about how to be a better mother (or a thinner, more fashionable or better-looking one). It's not just the celebrity mums pushing their prams on magazine covers, or the continuing dearth of mothers on television who are less than exceptionally good-looking, or that mothers in advertising remain ubiquitously obsessed with cleaning products and alpine-fresh scents. While television dramas have pleasingly increased the handful of roles that feature working mothers, the majority of them are unduly punished in the twists of the melodramatic plot. They have wimpy husbands or damaged children, and of course TV's bad characters are inevitably bad due to the shortcomings of their mothers (serial killers, for example, invariably have overbearing mothers or alcoholic mothers, or never really separated from their mothers).[2]

We are living, so it seems, in an age of overzealous motherhood. Indeed, in a world in which the demands of the workplace have increased, so too the ideals of motherhood have become paradoxically more – not less – demanding. In recent years, commonly accepted ideas about what constitutes a barely adequate level of mothering have drastically expanded to include extraordinary sacrifices of time, money, feelings, brains, social relationships and indeed sleep. In Australia, the majority of mothers work. But recent studies show that working mothers now spend more time with their children than their nonworking mothers did in 1975.[3] Working mothers achieve this extraordinary feat by sacrificing leisure, mental health, and even personal hygiene to spend more time with their kids. Back in the 1990s, sociologist Sharon Hays coined the term 'Intensive Mothering' to capture the cultural tensions and contradictions that have led to these extraordinary changes.[4]

Of course, it is not just an onslaught of seraphic images that is driving these transformations. There is also, for example, the welter of terrifying warnings. Every day, the shortcomings of delinquent mothers are broadcast on the television news – endless bulletins about mothers who lock their babies in their cars in the screaming heat, mothers who chain their toddlers to a cot, day care centres staffed by child molesters, orphanages crammed with abused and beaten children, preying paedophiles, child murderers and other nameless or unspeakable forms of abuse. Obviously, society needs to be active and vigilant in responding to criminality and neglect. But there is also a need to acknowledge that the sheer abundance of news calculated to instil white-knuckled horror into any self-respecting mother is historically and culturally specific, and has been escalating in Western nations since the 1980s.[5]

Nevertheless, it is not the horrifying warnings so much as it is a new kind of anxious sermonising that is having the most profound impact on mothers, especially among the middle class. This is the thesis explored in Élisabeth Badinter's book *The Conflict*, in which she argues that an ascendant ideology of 'Naturalism' has given rise to an industry of experts advocating increasingly pristine forms of natural birth and natural pregnancy, as well as an ever-expanding list of increasingly time-intensive child-rearing duties that (even in the face of feminist advances, or perhaps because of them) are deemed to fall to the mother alone. These duties include most of the classic practices of twenty-first-century child rearing, including such nostrums as co-sleeping, baby wearing and breastfeeding-on-demand until the age of two. Badinter argues that what is popularly called 'Naturalism' is in fact a resurgent ideological belief – driven by a range of economic imperatives – that women's 'Natural Place' is in the home.[6]

Whether it is called 'Intensive Mothering' or 'Natural Parenting', these new credos of motherhood are wholly taken up with the idea that there is a narrowly prescribed way of doing things. In the West, twenty-first-century child rearing is becoming increasingly time-consuming, expert-guided, emotionally all-absorbing and incredibly expensive. Moreover, in historical terms, I would be willing to hazard a guess that never before has motherhood been so heavily scrutinised. It is no longer just a question of whether you should or should not eat strawberries or prawns or soft cheese, or, heaven forbid, junk food, while you are pregnant, but so too, the issue of what you should or should not *feel* has come under intense scrutiny. Never before has there been such a microscopic investigation of a pregnant woman's emotional state, before, during and after birth. Indeed, the construction of new psychological disorders for mothers appears to have become something of a psychological pastime, with the old list of mental disorders expanding beyond prenatal anxiety, postnatal depression, postpartum psychosis and the baby blues, to include the baby pinks (a label for a woman who is illogically and inappropriately happy to be a mother), as well as prenatal and postnatal stress disorder, maternal anxiety and mood imbalance and tokophobia – the latter being coined at the start of this millennium as a diagnosis for an unreasonable fear of giving birth. In the 1970s, mothers in Australia blissfully fed their children on formula, tinned spaghetti and Tang – the chosen beverage of the astronauts. Today, women who are physically unable to breastfeed are endlessly lectured on their shortcomings, epidurals are tantamount to child abuse, and a medically assisted emergency delivery appears to have become a source of guilt and shame for some women.

The problem with the way in which this pop psychology is played out in the media is that it performs an endless re-inscription of the ideologies of mothering. These ideologies are often illogical, contradictory and – one suspects – more often dictated by what is convenient for society and not what is actually good for the children and parents involved. Hence, mothers should be young mothers (so their eggs are still fresh), but never too young (this would be a drain on the public purse), mothers should never be single mothers (they give birth to the criminals that swell the prison population) and should invariably be stay-at-home mothers (unless, of course, they are single mothers, in which case they should work). Above all else, mothers should be ecstatically happy mothers, because sad mothers are failed mothers. Indeed, according to the prevailing wisdom, unhappy mothers are downright unnatural – if not certifiably insane.[7]

Little wonder there has been an outcry against such miserable standards of perfection. The same decade that saw the seeming triumph of the ideologies of 'Intensive' and 'Natural' mothering, also saw the rise of what has been called the 'Parenting Hate Read'[8] – a popular outpouring of books and blogs written by mothers (and even a few fathers) who frankly confess that they are depressed about having children for no better reason than it is often mind-numbing, exhausting and dreadful. Mothers love their children, say the 'Parenting Hate Reads', but they do not like what is happening to their lives.

One of the first in the genre was Heather Armstrong's 'Dooce' blog, which went on to make Armstrong the twenty-sixth most influential woman in the American media, according to *Forbes* magazine. Dooce was quickly followed by the likes of Alice Bradley's 'Finslippy' and a plethora of lesser-known blogs such as 'Scary Mommy' and 'Rants from Mommyland'.[9] In Australia, they famously include 'Edenland' by mother, blogger, and self-confessed former alcoholic Eden Riley. But even a cursory reading of these blogs makes it abundantly clear that the 'Parenting Hate' tag is something of a misnomer because right on the coat-tails of even the most lurid accounts of the trials and tribulations of mothering, parenting blogs almost uniformly end with a ringing endorsement of children and family life. As it says on the blurb of Bradley's *Let's Panic About Babies!*, this manual will tell you, 'How to Endure and Possibly Triumph Over the Adorable Tyrant Who Will Ruin Your Body, Destroy Your Life, Liquefy Your Brain, and Finally Turn You Into a Worthwhile Human Being'.[10] In other words, mummy blogs are actually celebrating a picture of mothering that is chaotic, lifelike and down-to-earth.

The mainstream media has also cashed in on this trend, because, let's face it, mothers – whether they hate or love their lives – comprise a lucrative commercial market. In Argentina,

Coca-Cola ran an advertisement in which a toddler relentlessly destroys his parents' home, if not their entire lives, by depicting the kid's trash and dirty nappies piling up, and the green goo getting smeared over Dad's priceless LP collection. Of course, when the couple falls pregnant once again, they are overjoyed. In Europe, Fiat ran the 'Welcome to the Motherhood' promotion for the 500-litre family car, in which a fashionably dishevelled mother raps amidst the kids' toys and cornflakes on the living-room floor. Her life is a war of attrition against domestic mayhem and she's got the battle wounds to prove it, including an episiotomy scar and a nursing bra that she wears like a 'bulletproof vest'. This domestic reality tale is no doubt based on extensive focus group interviews, and obviously strikes a chord because it is clocking up the views on YouTube. I emailed the URL to a colleague, another working mum. 'I love it', she replied. Then added, 'I must be a horrible mother!' This got me thinking. The rise of the 'Parenting Hate' phenomenon might run counter to the myth of maternal bliss, but does it also run the risk of turning motherhood into a kind of misery competition?

The problem is perhaps only partly about the disparity between media images of ecstatically happy mummies and the reality of women's lives – it is also because our ideas about happiness have grown impoverished. Happiness, as it is commonly understood in the Western world, is made up of continuous moments of pleasure and the absence of pain. These popular assumptions about happiness are of comparatively recent origin, emerging in the works of philosophers such as Jeremy Bentham who argued – back in the eighteenth century – that people act purely in their self-interest and the goal to which self-interest aspires is happiness. Ethical conduct, according to Bentham and James Mill (father to John Stuart), should therefore aspire to maximise pleasure and minimise pain. Bentham and Mill were political progressives in their day, and their ambition to ameliorate the existence of their fellow human beings perhaps disguised – for a time, at least – the fact that utility and self-interest might not be all there is to goodness, or, indeed, all there is to happiness. Indeed, this ready equation of goodness, pleasure and happiness flew in the face of ideas that had been of concern to philosophers since Aristotle argued that a person is not made happy by fleeting pleasures, but by fulfilment stemming from meaning and purpose.[11] Or, as Nietzsche, the whirling dervish of nineteenth-century philosophy, put it, 'Man does not strive for happiness only the Englishman does.'[12]

Nevertheless, Western assumptions about happiness have remained broadly utilitarian, giving rise to a culturally constructed notion of happiness that readily transforms into television commercials showing families becoming happier with every purchase – or, indeed, by life coaches peddling the dubious hypothesis that self-belief can overcome the odds, whatever your social or economic circumstance. Barbara Ehrenreich remorselessly satirised these thinned-out notions of happiness in *Smile or Die*, an attack on positive psychology and acquisitive individualism.[13] More recently, Jennifer Senior queried the American obsession with measuring the happiness of mothers in particular, asking whether a narrowly determined idea of happiness is distorting the countless academic studies in which women have ranked childcare among the least pleasurable activities of their lives, below even housework.[14] One of the central problems with happiness studies as they are applied to public policy is that by focusing on individual and subjective 'feelings' they obscure the need to seek collective solutions to wider social problems, specifically by rearticulating social and economic problems as matters of personal 'attitude' or 'belief'. Indeed, should it come as such a surprise that in America, where there is no public healthcare, no statutory entitlement to maternity leave, and no government support for child care, mothers are more miserable – apparently – than elsewhere in the world?

Of course, there are additional cultural explanations for these statistical conundrums that might also be considered. High among them is the fact that for many women in the Western world the experience of raising children has fundamentally changed. Unless you are Mother Theresa, you have probably been spending your life up until the time you have kids in a reasonably independent and even self-indulgent way. You work hard through the week, but sleep in on the weekend. You go to parties. You come home drunk. You see your friends when you want. Babies have different ideas. They stick forks in electric sockets, go berserk in the back car seat, and throw up on your work clothes. They want to be carried around in the day and wake in the night. Babies challenge the central tenets of our liberal individualistic society and its endless privileging of 'me, me, me'. Put another way, as far as motherhood is concerned, what our impoverished idea of happiness fails to accommodate is the dirty little reality that the pleasures of mothers and children do not always coincide.

Nothing prepared me for being a mother. Nothing prepared me for the sleepless nights, the wild emotions, the fears and terrors that you have for your children. In *Motherhood*, Anne Manne bravely talks about the ways in which being a mother entails relationships and responsibilities that do not sit well with the individualistic language of late capitalism, and, indeed, some strands of feminism.[15] However, there is something deeply uncomfortable in the lessons that are so often extrapolated from the supposedly transformative power of a mother's love, especially when it is repositioned via safe-sounding catchphrases such as an 'ethic of care'. If a mother's love can be described as an ethic – which is arguable – then it is an ethic that excludes women who do not have children. It excludes men. It excludes teenagers and the elderly, and in many ways it excludes children, too. Indeed, it is precisely because mothering and loving do not come naturally or instinctively to many women that there is a need to talk about children. It may be a fallacy to understand children as resilient, fully independent creatures, as Manne argues. But it is equally false not to recognise the self-activity of children – that is, to understand children only as the passive recipients of mothering. Indeed, the great psychoanalyst Donald Winnicott, author of the theory of the 'Good Enough Mother', would, if he were alive today, surely have questioned the assumption that endless amounts of intensive mothering would help children to grow into autonomous, flourishing human beings.[16]

Women, as Badinter argues, are not chimpanzees. Yet Western ideas about motherhood are so often structured around deeply flawed arguments regarding what is 'Natural'. Of course, there is biology. But lives are also constructed through culture. If society can solve its social problems then maybe parenting will cease to be a misery competition – mothers might not be happy in a utilitarian or hedonistic sense, but will lead rich and satisfying lives – and then maybe a stay-at-home dad can change a nappy without a choir of angels descending from heaven singing 'Hallelujah'.

Endnotes

1   Numerous feminist scholars have produced work on the cultural ideology of the 'good mother'. For an excellent analysis, see S. Goodwin & K. Huppatz (eds), *The Good Mother: Contemporary Motherhoods in Australia*, Sydney University Press, 2010; and the earlier American classic S. Douglas & M. Michaels, *The Mommy Myth: The Idealisation of Motherhood and How it has Undermined all Women*, Simon and Schuster, New York, 2005.

2   For a recent analysis, see R. Feasey, *From Happy Homemaker to Desperate Housewives: Motherhood and Popular Television*, Anthem Press, 2012.

3   B. Pocock, N. Skinner & P. Williams (eds), *Time Bomb: Work, Rest and Play in Australia Today*, NewSouth, Sydney, 2012; L. Craig, *Contemporary Motherhood: the Impact of Children on Adult Time*, Ashgate, Aldershot, 2006.

4   S. Hays, *The Cultural Contradictions of Motherhood*, Yale University Press, 1996.

5   This media trend has been mapped by Douglas & Michaels, op. cit. See also C. Krinksky (ed.), *Moral Panics over Contemporary Children and Youth*, Ashgate, Farnham and Burlington, 2008; and M. De Young, *The Day Care Ritual Abuse Moral Panic*, McFarland, Jefferson, North Carolina, 2004.

6   E. Badinter, *The Conflict: Woman and Mother*, Text Publishing, Melbourne, 2011.

7   Contradictory ideologies of mothering are examined in Hays, op. cit. Goodwin & Huppatz, op. cit. See also D. Johnson & D. Swanson, 'Invisible Mothers: A content analysis of motherhood ideologies and myths in magazines,' *Sex Roles*, vol. 49, no. 1/2, 2003, pp. 21–33.

8   A. Hess, 'The Rise of the Parenting Hate Read,' Slate.com, 12 December 2013.

9   See M. Friedman & S. Caxite (eds), *Mothering and Blogging: The Radical Act of the Mommy Blog*, Demeter Press, 2009.

10   A. Bradley & E. Kennedy, *Let's Panic About Babies!*, St Martin's Press,

New York, 2011.

11 Aristotle, *The Nicomachean Ethics*, trans J. K. A. Thompson & H. Tredinnick, Penguin, [c 332 BC] 2004.

12 F. Nietzsche, *Twilight of the Idols*, in *Twilight of the Idols and the Anti Christ*, trans M. Tanner, Penguin, London, [1888] 1990, p. 33. On rethinking happiness, see M. Nussbaum, 'Who is the happy warrior? philosophy poses questions to psychology', *Journal of Legal Studies*, vol. 37, no. 2, 2008, pp. 81–113; and 'Who is the happy warrior? philosophy, happiness research, and public policy,' *International Review of Economics*, vol. 59, no. 4, 2012, pp. 335–61.

13 B. Ehrenreich, *Smile or Die: How Positive Thinking Fooled America and the World*, Granta, London, 2009.

14 J. Senior, *All Joy and No Fun: the Paradox of Modern Parenthood*, HarperCollins, New York, 2014. The Nobel Prize–winning behavioural economist Daniel Kahneman famously showed that parents report statistically significant lower levels of happiness than nonparents. See, D. Kahneman, A. B. Krueger, D. A. Schkade, N. Schwarz & A. A. Stone, 'A survey method for characterizing daily life experience: The day reconstruction method,' *Science*, vol. 306, 2004, pp. 1776–80. Their findings have been substantiated in other studies, see, for example, J. M. Twenge, W. K. Campbell & C. A. Foster, 'Parenthood and Marital Satisfaction', *Journal of Marriage and Family*, vol. 65, no. 3, 2003, pp. 574–83; and a recent British survey, J. Gabb, M. Klett-Davies, J. Fink & M. Thomae, *Enduring Love? Couple Relationships in the 21st Century, Survey Report Findings*, Open University, 2013.

15 A. Manne, *Motherhood: How Should We Care for Our Children?*, Allen & Unwin, Sydney, 2005.

16 D. W. Winnicott, *Playing and Reality*, Basic Books, New York, 1971; and D. W. Winnicott, *Babies and their Mothers*, Free Association Books, London, 1988. See also M. D. S. Ainsworth, M. Blehar & E. Waters, *Patterns of Attachment: A Psychological Study of the Strange Situation*, Lawrence Erlbaum, Hillsdale, NJ, 1978.

THE FOREST OR THE PIT?

Fossil Fuels, Climate Change and the Struggle for the Future Human Happiness[1]

David Ritter

In the ominous warmth of the early morning of a particularly ferocious Australian summer, the ants cast shadows. A dirt track runs down a long low hillside. At the top of the gentle incline is a farmhouse, accompanied by shady trees, a water tank, washing line and other signs of homely civility. At the foot of the slope, dust and stones line a waterless riverbed, flanked by gum trees on each bank. Farming this country, deep in the hinterland of New South Wales, has always been hard work; but the rains are perpetually overdue and the slog is getting crueller. A lonely generator gives off a constant drone. Yet for all the melancholy ambiance of struggle, the place is undeniably beautiful; an Australian rural idyll. But in the middle of one of the fields is something unexpected: a motley collection of twenty or so tents which sit like so many curious night beetles, made still by the dawn. As the light strengthens and the warming quickens, the sleepers awake and emerge, treading gingerly so as to avoid falling over ropes and pegs. One might be forgiven for imagining the gathering to be made up of lost vacationers, or maybe, in another age, colonials on the make. Instead, these men and women are patriots and pilgrims, drawn together in a heroic stand against a terrible threat. The hum and hubbub rise as the mundane business of first thing is undertaken; ablutions, mugs of tea or coffee, and breakfast. As the temperature begins to rise, people drink water conspicuously and bottles are filled prudentially for what lies ahead. Another big day beckons at Maules Creek in the Gunnedah Basin of central New South Wales, where a desperate contest over the future possibilities for human happiness is being duelled out under the wide southern sky.

Australia's largest coal mining company, Whitehaven, wants to dig a massive new mine at Maules Creek; the largest of its kind under construction anywhere in Australia. In order to do so, Whitehaven will have to clear swathes of the Leard State Forest, including areas of critically endangered box gum woodland. The inhabitants of what is now known as Camp Wando are determined that the mine will not go ahead. The stand-off has become known as the 'Leard Blockade'.

Historically, fossil fuels have been central to the enlargement of human happiness. Under any of the prevailing 'well-being' theories of happiness, all the commonly measured elements (positive emotion, engagement, relationships, meaning and purpose; and accomplishment) have been enabled on a vast scale by the increased prosperity made possible by the application of large-scale fossil fuel use.[2] Although there have always been egregious side effects, there is no doubt that development predicated on the extraction and application of easy energy sources in the centuries since the industrial revolution has brought radically increased life spans and better prospects for hundreds of millions of people. However, what we now know is that the extraordinary rise in standards of living has been enabled by the atmospheric equivalent of the picture of Dorian Gray. Every ounce of fossil fuel we have burned, and every tree we have felled in the pursuit of making things materially better for ourselves, has increased the amount of carbon dioxide in the atmosphere to a level unprecedented in human history.[3]

The consequences for the climate are now well known, albeit – and with great disingenuousness – disputed; the temperature will rise and extreme weather events will increase in frequency and intensity.[4] Already, global temperatures have increased by more than 1 degree celsius as a consequence of anthropogenic activity. In the future we can expect more melting of the polar ice, tundra and glaciers; rising sea levels; changes in the chemical composition and behaviour of our oceans, and the collapse of some terrestrial ecosystems.[5] We also risk radical nonlinear change as various transformations in the earth's surface may 'tip' the whole system out of control.[6] 'We are', a collection of Nobel Laureates wrote in a memorandum to the world's leaders, 'transgressing planetary boundaries that have kept civilization safe for the past 10,000 years'.[7] We are jeopardising the preconditions to all human happiness. Everything we've worked at, built or made; our poetry, justice, kindness and valour; each song sung, ball chased, tree climbed and picture painted; all homes made and journeys of discovery; every love any of us have ever had; the whole box and dice and tumble of what it means to be happy on earth, every bit of it has been enabled by a set of climactic conditions that are now at risk.

The links between climate change and happiness are increasingly coming to the attention of policymakers. This may seem counterintuitive: if happiness is a subjective feeling, it is probably not something policymakers are capable of doing much about. The emotional weather of one's inner world seems very far from the televised scenes of endless UN meetings of world leaders and technocratic talk about emissions quotas. This raises the perennial question of collective happiness: how can we even sensibly talk about the connections between happiness and collective decision-making? How do we quantify a subjective feeling in a way that it is a useful guide to making public-policy decisions?

A vast tradition of political and economic theory attempts to answer that question – from John Locke through Jeremy Bentham to modern welfare economics, by looking at 'objective' measures of human well-being – a tradition that it is beyond the scope of this essay to interrogate. The influence of that thinking, however, can be traced to much modern happiness theory, which assumes that there are both subjective and objective, internal and external, dimensions to happiness.[8] The 2012 *World Happiness Report*, published by the United Nations Sustainable Development Solutions Network, summarises that '[s]ome of the important external factors include income, work, community and governance, and values and religion. More "personal" factors include mental and physical health, family experience, education, gender, and age'.[9] The modern capabilities approach pioneered by Amartya Sen focuses on human 'welfare', rather than emotional happiness, defined through a list of objective capabilities.[10] This is not to negate the subjective aspects of happiness, it is merely to provide a list that can be assessed objectively, as a guide to making public decisions that maximise individual citizens' access to those components of happiness that collective decision-makers can do something about. No approach is perfect, but this author will assume that there is enough merit in objective approaches to render discussion of the connections between climate change and happiness worthwhile.

Drawing on this capability approach, the United Nations has increasingly included happiness – measured through objective lists of characteristics – in its indexes of human development.[11] In 2011 the United Nations General Assembly adopted a resolution (without a vote) noting that the GDP indicator 'does not adequately reflect the happiness and well-being of people in a country' and called on countries 'to pursue the elaboration of additional measures that better capture the importance of the pursuit of happiness and well-being in development with a view to guiding their public policies'.[12] UN agencies have begun using the Human Development Index to measure the effects of climate change on human welfare or happiness. This enabled the United Nations Development Programme, in collaboration with the government of Bhutan, to state in 2011 that 'Climate change threatens Bhutan's Gross National Happiness' because of the effects of changing weather patterns and melting glaciers on the vulnerable one quarter of Bhutan's population living in poverty, dependent on subsistence farming and local natural resources'.[13]

The 2012 *World Happiness Report* stated that climate change was one of the biggest risks to the overall development of happiness, saying, 'Most importantly, the lifestyles of the rich imperil the survival of the poor. Human-induced climate change is already hitting the poorest regions and claiming lives and livelihoods'.[14] A Spanish study found that '[n]ot applying environmental policies to mitigate climate change can have negative consequences when it comes to happiness', as 'being exposed to extreme climate experiences, such as forest fires or flooding, phenomena which could occur more frequently in the most common scenarios of climate change, have considerable and lasting negative effects on the wellbeing and happiness of individuals'.[15] The authors of the *World Happiness Report* conclude, 'The quest for happiness will be carried out in the context of growing environmental risks.'[16] Ross Garnaut has described Australia as 'being the developed nation that is expected to be most badly affected by unmitigated climate change'.[17] According to Garnaut, '[i]f global development continues without effective mitigation, the mainstream science tells us that the impacts of climate change on Australia are likely to be severe.'[18]

In order to limit climate change – no more than 2 degrees remains the extant international target – it will be necessary to shift the global economy to a low-carbon pathway, including rapid transitioning to renewable energy. It is a historic inflection point in which the great public policy imperative to reduce greenhouse gas emissions is in conflict with deeply vested political economy.[19] Ideationally, the longstanding notion that cheap fossil-fuel-based energy will increase the quantum of human happiness has collided with the new conclusion that in order to secure our future prosperity, we must shift quickly to new energy sources. Paradoxically, we seem to be both accepting the case for change and giving in to the status quo. As the economist Martin Wolf has written:

> The world has got itself into an extremely contradic-
> tory place. Governments have committed themselves
> to a view of the risks of climate change. That view
> implies a rapid revolution in the energy mix and
> correspondingly rapid reductions in emissions of

greenhouse gases. But major energy producers do not believe governments will do what they promise. They envisage a very different and quite unrevolutionary energy future in which the reserves they now possess and those they plan to develop will all be burnt.[20]

The sharp edges of the contradiction are at the sites of starkest choice. Coal offers the greatest incongruity of all. Measured in conventional economic terms (that is, by not counting the externalities), coal is the cheapest fossil fuel, but it is also the dirtiest and makes the single greatest contribution to rising carbon emissions globally.[21] The world's most famous climate scientist, Professor James Hansen, has been extraordinarily blunt on the subject of coal, writing that:

> [C]oal is the single greatest threat to civilisation and all life on our planet.... [I]t is not only the largest fossil fuel reservoir of carbon dioxide, it is the dirtiest fuel. Coal is polluting the world's oceans and streams with mercury, arsenic and other dangerous chemicals...The trains carrying coal to power plants are death trains. Coal-fired power plants are factories of death.[22]

In response, coal industry advocates insist that their product continues to remain essential to increasing the sum total of human happiness, by creating employment,[23] through generating taxes and royalties to governments that pay for essential services,[24] as an export earner that increases national prosperity,[25] and by alleviating poverty through the provision of affordable energy.[26] In 2014, the world's largest coal company, Peabody, embarked on an aggressive promotional campaign, extolling the virtue of coal as a means of lifting the immiserated from poverty:

Access to electricity fuels progress and drives health and longevity. Yet today, more than half of the people across the globe lack proper electricity, and another 2 billion people will require power as the population grows. This means that as many as 5 billion to 6 billion people will lack proper energy in as little as two decades. We have the power to solve this crisis.[27]

Coal, fuel of death; coal, bringer of life – the disjunction over coal's relationship to our future happiness could not be more profound.

In an Australian context the disjointed nature of things is plain. The Australian government is committed to the international target of restricting climate change to no greater than 2 degrees of warming and has received extensive expert advice on the consequences of failing to do so,[28] but extant plans to exploit the nation's coal reserves are thoroughly inconsistent with that desperately pragmatic goal. Hansen has said that kicking the coal habit 'is the greatest gift Australians could give to everybody's children, future generations, and other life on our planet'.[29] Between 1986 and 2012 Australia was the world's number one coal exporter, and now sits second behind Indonesia. No Australian government agency or industry body even tracks the amount of carbon that will be emitted when coal excavated in our country is burned in power stations overseas. There are eighty new coal projects or extensions that are currently planned, but the law does not require any regard to be had for the climate change implications of the commodity being used as intended.[30] In an address in which the coal industry was singled out for praise, Prime Minister Tony Abbott – who at least rhetorically is committed to action on climate change – described Australia's 'destiny' as bringing 'affordable energy to the world'.[31] Ostensible commitment to the imperatives of climate science and the gravity of prevailing political economy exist simultaneously. The incongruity has been noticed. In an essay reflecting on the politics of coal Down Under, Bill McKibben observed that '[o]fficial Australia seems to be stuck in a bizarre state of denial, the kind where you acknowledge that you have a problem, but not that you need to do anything about it'.[32]

There are various ways of responding to a contradiction. In relation to the persistence and expansion of coal usage and the repercussions for the climate, the plunging coal price is helping to derail and delay numerous projects (though not Maules Creek at this stage), but without additional action the economics alone will be insufficient to finally deal with the problem.[33] The most infamous means of 'resolving' the quandary, of course, is by simply denying that global warming is real (or, if conceding that the climate is changing, then refusing to accept that the cause is anthropogenic).[34] However, despite the innuendo and dog whistling, and notwithstanding whatever conversations might go on behind closed doors, overt rejection of climate science remains a minority position and one that will deservedly attract controversy and opprobrium.

Instead of publically debating the science, the coal industry has by and large turned to a second method of resolving the contradiction; squaring the circle by declaring the future to be in 'clean coal' or 'sustainable coal'. What the coal industry has meant by 'clean coal' has fluctuated over time – from the superior quality of Australian coal and extraction techniques, to research into the application of carbon capture and storage – but the legitimising function of the alliterative slogan has remained constant. For politicians in particular, 'clean coal' offers a way of rhetorically accepting the climate science while not having to do anything about the primary driver. Better still, for those committed to a line of animated inaction then if coal is 'clean', hey presto, the black stuff can even be touted as part of the solution. As the Cohen Brothers memorably observed through a short campaign video released in 2009, 'clean coal harnesses the awesome power of the word "clean" to make it sound like the cleanest clean there is'.[35] In one instance, the primacy of discursive function over physical substance became so plain that an Australian government fund set up to assist the industry to technologically develop 'clean coal' was used to market the benefits of the industry instead.[36] Whatever the rhetorical effect, none of the technically possible 'clean coal' fixes that have been touted appear feasible at scale.[37] As Pearse, McKnight and Burton summarise in their 2013 study *Big Coal*:

> The lesson from what we've seen is pretty clearly that coal can't be clean, no matter how hard the industry tries to persuade us otherwise, and no matter how much we might want to believe them.[38]

Yet still the language persists. Whitehaven Coal is certainly well-versed in the coal industry's cultivated doublespeak. The company 'is committed', the Whitehaven corporate website pledges in vivid blue tautology, 'to the sustainable development of its coal reserves'.[39] The claim is doubly perverse in the case of Whitehaven and Maules Creek, because quite apart from the question of carbon emissions, the mine requires destruction of large sections of the Leard Forest, including a critically endangered ecosystem and habitat for at least thirty threatened species. Whitehaven were able to obtain permission to engage in the destruction of parts of the Leard Forest because of promises made to secure and protect ecologically equivalent areas, a practice known as 'offsetting'. Although Whitehaven's plan has so far survived legal challenge, significant doubts remain about the ecological validity of the proposed offsetting.[40] In another episode, Whitehaven obtained special permission to destroy forest in winter – a practice normally forbidden because hibernating animals have no chance to escape. Part of Whitehaven's response was to state that they would be 'gently' bulldozing trees.[41] According to former Australian Deputy Prime Minister Mark Vaile who is now Chairman of Whitehaven, the company is 'running a sustainable business within a sustainable industry'.[42]

Out at Camp Wando, nobody is inclined to believe a word that Whitehaven says. Although it is a heterogeneous crowd, much of the protest comes from local people who dispute Whitehaven's claims and for whom the abstract promises about the 'economic benefits of the coal industry' matter little in the face of the defilement and destruction of the places they love. The felicitously cheerful Ros Druce, for example, grew up on a farm a mere 4 kilometres from the planned mine site, and was arrested for the first time in April 2014.[43] Then there is the owner of the property on which the Maules Creek protest camp is located, a big bloke called Cliff Wallace, older than seventy, who has farmed the area for almost three decades and is emphatic that he is 'doing the right thing' by making his land available for the struggle.[44] The Laird family, whose name is given – albeit in different spelling – to the Leard State Forest, have farmed the nearby country for five generations and are also prominent among the leadership of the resistance to the mine. In January 2014, family spokesman Phil Laird (another big bloke, with a king-size hat and a voice to match) wrote that:

> [i]n the battle that is gripping my community this coming Australia Day, my fifth generation farming family and I are siding with the underdogs against Big Coal…. Having exhausted all official avenues, we are rising up as a community this Australia Day weekend and putting ourselves on the line to blockade the mine site.[45]

In the early part of 2014 Phil Laird and others signed a document believed to be unique in Australian history, pledging mutual support with the local traditional owners, the Gomeroi people, in resisting the development.[46] The Gomeroi are also largely opposed to the construction of the mine because Whitehaven has ignored two decades of industry best practice and failed to reach a proper land use agreement.[47] The Gomeroi allege specific disrespect to their culture including destruction of sites of significance; a grievance that is both distinct from and intimately entwined with the wider Maules Creek dispute.

Others, though, come from outside, some of whom are motivated to acts of conscience by contemplation of the meaning of climate change or deep love of nature.[48] Some speak of a kind of fulfilment that is met through acting in accordance with the stirrings of conscience. Thea Ormerod is the president of the Australian Religious Response to Climate Change. She is an earnest, silvery-haired grandmother, a woman of faith and enormous character. 'We cannot with any integrity', Thea wrote in 2009, 'profess to honour the Creator and then trash Creation'.[49] Five years later and Thea and the ARRCC have become heavily involved in the campaign to stop the Maules Creek mine. Thea herself was eventually arrested, having taken part in a multifaith prayer vigil at one of the entry points to the Maules Creek mine site.[50] A photograph captures the moment after her seizure, as a composed Thea sits peacefully inside the back of the police wagon, squinting against the harsh light, with a large crucifix necklace resting on her plain white blouse.[51]

Another unlikely protestor is Bill Ryan, a 93-year-old veteran of the Kokoda campaign, arguably Australia's most significant campaign of World War II, who is now legally blind. More Australian lives were lost in the course of Kokoda than any other campaign in the conflict and the Imperial Japanese army came closer to the Australian mainland than at any other point. More than sixty years later, Bill has been arrested twice up at Maules Creek, defying police requests to leave the protest line. Justifying his actions, Bill wrote:

> I've only got a few years left, but I feel in my con-
> science that I have to take this stand... Something
> is wrong. We're faced with a catastrophe. I owe it to

my grandchildren, and I owe it to all children. I was willing to put my life on the line in the Second World War, so putting my body on the line here is a small inconvenience.[52]

Other opponents of the Maules Creek mine have seen similar parallels. Writing before she and her husband set off to 'enlist' in the protest for the first time, 73-year-old Robin Mosman identified 'ordinary Australians standing against the mining companies' as the country's patriotic soldiers of today.[53] There have now been more than 240 arrests for acts of peaceful civil disobedience as people resist the clearing of the Leard Forest and the construction of the mine.

The Leard Blockade is a dispute over both the status of truth and the future of happiness. It is both a flashpoint in a truly global crisis and a deeply local struggle by people frantic to save their homes and way of life and work. Perhaps environmental politics at its most kinetic always comes from the merging of the streams of romance and reason focused on the tangibly particular. These are the moments when the thread of meaning between the chemical composition of the atmosphere and the existential ache for green space, clean water and the sound of the birds becomes iridescent.

Rising in a helicopter above the Gunnedah Basin, the physical manifestations of the contest over human happiness are inscribed plainly in the land. A bird's-eye view allows ready comprehension of the scale of the damage that coal has already inflicted on this region, as numerous existing mines gape greyly from the earth. And now a new cut is made. Despite the best efforts of the men and women of Camp Wando, first coal has been mined. The dark pit is beginning to open. Whether the project can be stopped before the destruction is complete and the climate change potential of Maules Creek is unleashed, remains in the balance, as do the conditions for the future happiness of our species.

Endnotes

1   It should be acknowledged at the outset that the author is not a
disinterested observer, but an active and partisan participant in the
politics described in this essay. The author would like to thank the
editors of this volume for their patience and the anonymous referees
for their suggestions. The author would also like to thank Jessica
Panegyres and Julie Macken for their specific help and assistance.

2   See generally M. E. P. Seligman, *Authentic Happiness: Using the New
Positive Psychology to Realize Your Potential for Lasting Fulfillment*, Free
Press/Simon and Schuster, New York, 2002.

3   The concentration of carbon dioxide in the atmosphere passed 400
parts per million for the first time in human history in May 2013.

4   The authoritative guide to climate change remains the work of
the International Panel on Climate Change: http://www.ipcc.ch/.
In Australia, regard should be had to the impact reports regularly
produced by the Climate Council: https://www.climatecouncil.org.
au/. The seminal work in relation to the constructed and disingenuous
nature of climate scepticism is N. Oreskes & E. M. Conway, *Merchants
of Doubt: How a Handful of Scientists Obscured the Truth on Issues from
Tobacco Smoke to Global Warming*, Bloomsbury Press, 2010. For a
typology of climate scepticism, see C. Hamilton, *Requiem for a Species:
Why We Resist the Truth about Climate Change*, Earthscan, 2010.

5   These and other effects are described in the various IPCC reports. See
note 4.

6   In relation to tipping points, see T. M. Lenton, H. Held, E. Kriegler,
J. W. Hall, W. Lucht, S. Rahmstorf, H. J. Schellnhuber, 'Inaugural
Article: Tipping elements in the Earth's climate system', *Proceedings of
the National Academy of Sciences*, vol. 105, no. 6, 2008, p. 1786.

7   'The Stockholm Memorandum. Tipping the Scales towards sustainability', May 2011, 3rd Nobel Laureate Symposium on Global Sustainability, Stockholm, Sweden, 16–19 May 2011.

8   See for example, B. S. Frey & A. Stutzer, *Happiness and Economics: How the Economy and Institutions Affect Human Well-being*, Princeton University Press, New Jersey, 2002, p. 20.

9   J. Helliwell, R. Layard & J. Sachs, United Nations Sustainable Development Solutions Network, *World Happiness Report*, 2012, 'Introduction', p. 9.

10 A. Sen, *Development as Freedom*, Oxford University Press, Oxford New York, 2001.

11 United Nations Development Program, Human Development Index reports available at http://hdr.undp.org/en/content/human-development-index-hdi.

12 'Happiness should have greater role in development policy – UN Member States', UN News Centre, 19 July 2011, http://www.un.org/apps/news/story.asp?NewsID=39084#.VCTEpRaoqSo.

13 'Climate change threatens Bhutan's Gross National Happiness', United Nations Development Programme Media Release, 1 September 2011, http://www.undp.org/content/undp/en/home/presscenter/pressreleases/2011/09/01/bhutan-s-gross-national-happiness-threatened-by-climate-change/.

14 *World Happiness Report*, 'Introduction', p. 5.

15 F. Sekulova & J. C. J. M. van den Bergh, 'Climate change, income and happiness: An empirical study for Barcelona', *Global Environmental Change*, vol. 23, no. 6, 2013, p. 1467. The quote was taken from an interview with the author, published in Universitat Autònoma de Barcelona. 'Happiness and mitigation of climate change: Economic degrowth compatible with wellbeing if work stability is maintained', *ScienceDaily*, 12 March 2014, http://www.sciencedaily.com/releases/2014/03/140312132353.htm.

16 *World Happiness Report*, 'Introduction', p. 7.

17 The Garnaut Climate Change Review Update 2011, http://www.garnautreview.org.au/update-2011/garnaut-review-2011/chapter3.html.

18 R. Garnaut, *The Garnaut Climate Change Review: Final Report*, Cambridge University Press, Melbourne, 2008, p. 125.

19 K. Taft, 'Fossil Fuels, Global Warming and Democracy: A Report from a Scene of the Collision', *Perspectives*, Whitlam Institute, Sydney, September 2014.

20 M. Wolf, 'A Climate Fix would ruin Investors', *Financial Times*, 17

June 2014, http://www.ft.com/cms/s/0/5a2356a4-f58e-11e3-afd3-00144feabdc0.html#axzz3EQJxKyCN.

21 D. Helm, *The Carbon Crunch: How We're Getting Climate Change Wrong – and How to Fix it*, Yale, 2012, p. 38.

22 J. Hansen, 'Coal-fired power stations are death factories. Close them', *Observer*, 15 February 2009, http://www.guardian.co.uk/commentisfree/2009/feb/15/james-hansen-power-plants-coal.

23 See the 'coal' page of the Minerals Council of Australia website, http://www.minerals.org.au/resources/coal/national_dividends_of_a_strong_coal_industry.

24 See for example, the arguments of the Minerals Council of Australia at http://www.minerals.org.au/resources/coal/taxes_and_royalties. This is the logic behind Queensland Premier Campbell Newman's argument: 'We are in the coal business. If you want decent hospitals, schools and police on the beat we all need to understand that', http://www.news.com.au/national/unesco-slams-great-barrier-reef-management-youve-got-eight-months-to-fix-it/story-e6frfkw0-1226381188474.

25 See the Minerals Council of Australia, http://www.minerals.org.au/resources/coal/national_dividends_of_a_strong_coal_industry.

26 See the arguments of the Minerals Council of Australia in this regard at http://www.minerals.org.au/resources/coal/coal_bringing_power_to_the_people. See also B. Pearson, 'Coal the answer to energy poverty', *The Drum*, 8 April 2014, http://www.abc.net.au/news/2014-04-08/pearson-coal-the-answer-to-energy-poverty/5371462.

27 See http://www.peabodyenergy.com/content/491/Advocating-Coals-Role-Alleviating-Energy-Poverty-to-the-Worlds-Energy-Ministers.

28 The Climate Commission was an independent body established in 2011 by the Federal Government of Australia to communicate 'reliable and authoritative information' about climate change in Australia. It was abolished by the Abbott Government in September 2013 and then privately relaunched as an independent nonprofit organisation known as the Climate Council: https://www.climatecouncil.org.au/about-us. The CSIRO publishes an annual 'State of the Climate' report to provide a 'summary of observations of Australia's climate and analysis of the factors that influence it', http://www.csiro.au/Outcomes/Climate/Understanding.aspx.

29 J. Hansen, NASA's Goddard Institute for Space Studies, quoted in G. Pearse, D. McKnight & B. Burton, *Big Coal*, NewSouth Publishing, Coogee, 2013.

30 J. Barber, K. Penney, T. Shael, S. Cowling & P. Nicholson, *Resources and Energy Major Projects October 2013*, Bureau of Resources and Energy Economics, Canberra, November 2013.

31 T. Abbott, 'Address to the Minerals Week 2014 Annual Minerals Industry Parliamentary Dinner', 28 May 2014, Canberra: http://www.scribd.com/doc/226734055/14-05-28-Address-to-the-Minerals-Week-2014-Annual-Minerals-Industry-Parliamentary-Dinner-Canberra. It should be noted though, that while Labor is currently out of power everywhere but South Australia and Victoria, the ALP is in virtual lock-step with the Coalition in supporting coal. On the other side of the big party divide, the Australian Labor Party's record is scarcely better when it comes to giving coal miners what they want. When introducing the carbon tax legislation in 2011, Greg Combet said that '[t]he simple fact is that the coal industry has a very bright future in Australia and will be supported.' The Hon Greg Combet, 'Gillard Government supports coal mining jobs', 18 July 2011 Media Release, http://www.climatechange.gov.au/ministers/hon-greg-combet-am-mp/media-release/gillard-government-supports-coal-mining-jobs. As to what Abbott really believes about climate change, see G. Readfern, 'What does Australian prime minister Tony Abbott really think about climate change?', *Guardian*, 16 June 2014, http://www.theguardian.com/environment/planet-oz/2014/jun/16/what-does-australian-prime-minister-tony-abbott-really-think-about-climate-change.

32 B. McKibben, 'False Profits: How australian coal is causing global damage', *Monthly*, June 2013, http://www.themonthly.com.au/issue/2013/june/1370181600/bill-mckibben/how-australian-coal-causing-global-damage.

33 In short, because the declining coal price is not, of course, causing less coal to be burned.

34 See C. Hamilton, note 4.

35 S. Goldberg, 'Coen brothers target US coal industry', *Guardian*, 27 Feb 2009, http://www.theguardian.com/environment/2009/feb/26/coen-brothers-coal-industry-film.

36 See '"Clean coal" money used to promote coal use', http://www.abc.net.au/lateline/content/2013/s3787338.htm.

37 'The fuel of the future, unfortunately', *Economist*, 19 April 2014, http://www.economist.com/news/business/21600987-cheap-ubiquitous-and-flexible-fuel-just-one-problem-fuel-future.

38 G. Pearse, D. McKnight & B. Burton, *Big Coal*.

39 http://www.whitehavencoal.com.au/environment.cfm

40 The validity of the offsetting remains bitterly contested. See
the variety of views expressed in the Commonwealth Senate
Standing Committee on Environment and Communications
Report into the effectiveness of Environmental Offsets, with
specific regard to Whitehaven Coal's Maules Creek Project, http://
www.aph.gov.au/Parliamentary_Business/Committees/Senate/
Environment_and_Communications/Environmental_Offsets/Report/
index.

41 P. Hannam, 'Whitehaven backdown on winter clearing in Maules
Creek a massive win, says community group', *Sydney Morning
Herald*, 12 June 2014, http://www.smh.com.au/environment/
whitehaven-backdown-on-winter-clearing-in-maules-creek-a-
massive-win-says-community-group-20140612-zs5wq.html. The
relevant biodiversity management plan stated: 'Use a bulldozer to start
pushing the tree over. Move the bulldozer over the roots and continue
gently pushing the tree over. The tree should not fall heavily to the
ground'.

42 Whitehaven Annual Report, 2013, p.7, http://www.whitehavencoal.
com.au/investors/documents/WhitehavenCoalLimited_
AnnualReport2013.pdf.

43 S. Trenoweth, 'Leard coalmine protest brings out young and old',
Saturday Paper, 12 April 2014, http://www.thesaturdaypaper.com.au/
news/environment/2014/04/12/leard-coalmine-protest-brings-out-
young-and-old/1397224800#.U8PNx7Hq2ZQ.

44 M. Safi, 'Narrabri farmer goes in to bat for coalmine protesters',
Guardian, 6 March 2014, http://www.theguardian.com/world/2014/
mar/06/narrabri-farmer-goes-into-bat-coalmine-protesters.

45 P. Laird, 'This Australia day, us underdogs will fight Big Coal to save
Maules Creek', *Guardian*, 24 January 2014, http://www.theguardian.
com/commentisfree/2014/jan/24/this-australia-day-us-underdogs-
will-fight-big-coal-to-save-maules-creek.

46 The full text of the 'Leard Forest Alliance and Gomeroi Traditional
Owners Protection Treaty' is available online at http://www.
lockthegate.org.au/leard_forest_protection_treaty.

47 O. Laughland, 'Maules Creek coal mine divides local
families and communities', *Guardian*, 9 April 2014, http://
www.theguardian.com/environment/2014/apr/09/
maules-creek-mine-divides-families-and-communities.

48 Greenpeace committed to the campaign to prevent the
    Maules Creek coal mine from being constructed in late 2013.
    See D. Ritter, 'An open letter to NSW farmer Phil Laird:
    Greenpeace stands with you', *Guardian*, 12 December 2013,
    http://www.theguardian.com/commentisfree/2013/dec/12/
    an-open-letter-to-nsw-farmer-phil-laird-greenpeace-stands-by-you.
49 'Earth Hour Address by ARRCC's Thea Ormerod', 31 March 2009,
    http://www.arrcc.org.au/earth-hour-address-by-arrccs-thea-ormerod.
50 R. Tyson, 'Protesters aim to get divine intervention
    over coalmine', *Northern Daily Leader*, 13 March 2014,
    http://www.northerndailyleader.com.au/story/2146696/
    protesters-aim-to-get-divine-intervention-over-coalmine/.
51 The image has been widely circulated. See http://www.greenpeace.
    org/australia/en/news/climate/Prayer-Vigil-at-Maules-Creek-Mine/.
    The photographer was Tom Jefferson, a man whose images have been
    seminal to bringing the Maules Creek dispute to life. Tom died in
    a tragic accident while on assignment in Scandinavia in mid-2014,
    leaving a partner and young family.
52 B. Ryan, 'At 92, I was arrested for protesting against mining. I'm glad
    I took a stand', *Guardian*, 1 April 2014, http://www.theguardian.com/
    commentisfree/2014/apr/01/at-92-i-was-arrested-for-protesting-
    against-mining-im-glad-i-took-a-stand.
53 R. Mosman, 'We're signing up for active duty', http://francesjones.
    wordpress.com/2014/06/01/were-signing-up-for-active-duty/.

PURSUING HAPPINESS: THE POLITICS OF SURVIVING WELL TOGETHER

J. K. Gibson-Graham, Jenny Cameron and Stephen Healy

Until recently, it has been widely assumed that economic measures such as Gross Domestic Product and Gross National Product gauge not just the economic well-being of nations but the subjective well-being – the happiness – of their citizens. However, over the last forty years this assumption has been unravelling as studies investigate the empirical link between economic development and happiness. In 1974, Richard Easterlin compared data from countries across the globe and his findings have become known as the Easterlin paradox: *within* countries, those on higher incomes are happier than those on lower incomes; however, when comparisons are made *between* countries there is little difference in levels of happiness between richer and poorer countries, and as countries get richer levels of happiness do not necessarily increase.[1]

With more data now available, the Easterlin paradox has been refined and researchers pinpoint that once Gross Domestic Product per capita reaches $15,000 per year there is no system-atic relationship between levels of happiness and Gross Domestic Product.[2] Indeed, in some so–called advanced economies such as the UK and the US, levels of happiness have decreased as Gross Domestic Product has increased.[3]

Alongside studies that unsettle and even overturn the presumed relationship between happiness and economic advancement, there is growing interest in devising indicators that de-economise happiness by incorporating the full range of factors that are thought to play a role in shaping well-being and happiness. In 1972, the fourth King of Bhutan, His Majesty Jigme Singye Wangchuck, provocatively pronounced that 'Gross National Happiness is more important than Gross Domestic Product'.[4] Building on this commitment, the government of Bhutan has devised an index for measuring Gross National Happiness based on nine domains, of which economic development (expressed as living standards) is only one. Other indicators that delink happiness from economic advancement include the New Economics Foundation's Happy Planet Index and the United Nations World Happiness Report.[5] These new measures are part of a critical interrogation of the notion of 'development' that highlights the short-term and limited priorities (and perverse outcomes) that emerge when development is understood simply as economic success. These measures expand the conception of development to include not only human happiness and but also planetary health.

The critical role that measures such as Gross National Happiness, Happy Planet Index and the World Happiness Report have played in debates about human and planetary well-being are welcome, if not long overdue. One important aspect of these measures is that they move away from understanding happiness in purely individualised terms as a personality trait, and acknowledge the role that collective endeavours play. Another is the way they incorporate an expanded understanding of the economy as involving not just familiar economic activities, but also hidden economic activities such as unpaid and volunteer work. However, there is a troubling side to their deployment. By reducing happiness to a single national measure and even ranking countries according to their happiness score, these indicators replicate some of the more concerning features of individually oriented understandings of happiness. This chapter explores other ways that measurement tools might be used to enable more politically engaged futures.

Beyond an Individualised Approach

One characteristic of the emerging national measures of happiness is their acknowledgement that happiness is a collective endeavour. In Bhutan the founding view is that it is not sufficient to focus narrowly 'on happiness that begins and ends with oneself and is concerned for and with oneself' because '[t]he pursuit of happiness is collective'.[6] This recognition of the collective or relational aspect of happiness is reflected in the Gross National Happiness index, most explicitly via the domains of community vitality (which includes social supports and community relationships), cultural diversity (which includes socio-cultural participation) and good governance (which includes political participation and political freedom). However, other domains also recognise collective endeavours. For example, the domain of time use includes unpaid and volunteer work that contributes to families and communities. Even the domain of ecological diversity and resilience takes a collective view by including people's sense of responsibility towards the environment, thus acknowledging the importance of human and nonhuman relationships. Other national measures also recognise that relations with others matter. For example, the United Nations World Happiness Report includes the role of social support (expressed as having someone to count on in times of trouble) and the prevalence of generosity (expressed as giving money to charity).

As it turns out, relations with others might not just be about individual, family, neighbourhood or community-based practices. According to the 2013 World Happiness Report the five happiest countries were Denmark, Norway, Switzerland, Netherlands and Sweden, all nations that systematically invest in schemes for assuring collective well-being. This result certainly seems to challenge the tenets of neoliberal government that promote individualism, austerity and disinvestment in social welfare as the rightful way to progress the nation. It might be that a strong sense of collectivity enacted through both informal and day-to-day practices of caring and giving, and more formal mechanisms of government are indispensable to securing happiness and well-being.

Beyond a Familiar Economic Approach

The emerging national measures of happiness don't just challenge the assumption that economic advancement secures happiness, they also challenge understandings of economy. Generally the economy is narrowly understood as involving paid workers employed in capitalist enterprises to produce goods and services that are sold in the market. However, as noted above, the national measures take into account other forms of work, such as the unpaid and volunteer work that occurs in households and communities, as well as acts of giving. Elsewhere, we have used the image of the diverse economy iceberg to capture this expanded understanding of economy (see Figure 8.1).

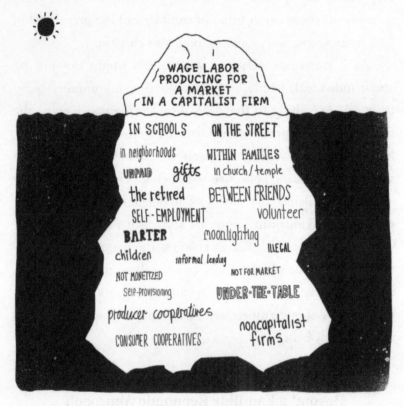

Figure 8.1: The Diverse Economy Iceberg

The emphasis on economic advancement as the route to happiness largely focuses on that small fraction of the diverse economy iceberg that sits above the waterline. Whereas the emerging national measures of happiness suggest that there are many more economic practices that contribute to happiness. Indeed, the 2013 World Happiness Report notes that volunteering, donating to charity and helping a stranger are all associated with higher individual levels of happiness.[7] Thinking about the economy in this way also has implications for environmental well-being. As identified in the introduction, there is a level of national economic development needed to secure well-being (pinpointed at a Gross Domestic Product per capita of $15,000 per year), but economic development beyond this level does not guarantee happiness. In a climate-changing world, there is the risk that if happiness is aligned purely with economic development, understood as increasing levels of production and consumption, this will further undermine the very environmental conditions that make life (as we know it) possible on this planet. Whereas economic development, defined as diversifying economic practices, particularly focusing on activities with a low carbon footprint, may well be key to both human and planetary well-being.

The Downside of Happiness Indicators

Measuring happiness at a national level is part of a larger trend of using statistical indicators to, as Sally Engle Merry puts it, 'measure the world'.[8] The attraction of indicators is their power 'to convert complicated and contextually variable phenomenon into unambiguous, clear, and impersonal measures'.[9] Thus a single number can stand as an accurate account of a nation's happiness and be used for comparing and ranking nations according to their level of happiness. One effect of the reliance on indicators to make a complicated world both knowable and manageable is that technical and statistical expertise comes to the fore, and provides the means for supposedly objective and rational decision-making. As a result, '[i]ndicators replace judgments on the basis of values or politics'.[10] A second effect is that nations are depicted as coherent wholes and the diversity of individuals and circumstances within nations is overridden.[11] Thus social scientists such as John Law call for 'an alternative sensibility' that recognises the complexity of any given context and uses more qualitative methods such as interviews, focus groups and citizens' juries to reveal the heterogeneity of a collective such as a nation.[12]

This alternative sensibility is evident in a recent Australian effort to define what Australians consider the key dimensions of 'progress', particularly with the aim of taking into account not just the economic but also the social, environmental and governance dimensions of progress.[13] The Measures of Australia's Progress project, run by the Australian Bureau of Statistics over two years (2011 and 2012), asked a broad range of Australians, 'What is important to you for national progress?'[14] Consultation methods included workshops, forums and social media (such as blogs and Facebook). The project identified twenty-three aspirations that are important to Australians. Contradictions are readily apparent. Australians 'want their environment to become healthier rather than degraded over time',[15] yet they also want increased well-being 'understood as having the opportunities, means and ability to have a high standard of living and lead the kind of life they want and choose to live'.[16] They aspire to a growing economy with quality paid employment, yet they would like to have the availability of time for 'building and maintaining positive relationships'.[17] We might conclude, as did some members of the popular press when the report was published, that Australians want to 'have it all' and are unable to let go of anything. It seems that there is work to be done if an alternative sensibility is to generate outcomes that can contribute to meaningful discussions, debates and decision-making.

Toward a 'Relational Metrics' Approach

Indicators have the potential to be developed beyond mere end points for projects aiming to establish levels of happiness. They can be the starting point for conversations about the means of attaining happiness. In what follows, we discuss a series of what we call 'relational metrics' that offer examples of the sorts of indicators that might be used as prompts for these conversations about means.[18] The idea with relational metrics is to highlight the collective nature of happiness and well-being, and the role that an economy comprised of diverse economic practices can play in attaining happiness and well-being. We apply these metrics to two lives that are based on real people. To begin, let's replace the idea of the pursuit of happiness with the pursuit of 'surviving well together'. Surviving well together is a collective endeavour engaging multiple elements – individual happiness and well-being, and the happiness and well-being of others and the planet on which we live. The term survival might seem too linked to material sufficiency, but for us it gestures towards the maintenance of life conjuring up the human and nonhuman others that contribute to this delicately balanced process.

Our relational metrics start by exploring individual happiness and well-being via a 24-hour time-use clock on which to record hours of work, rest and play. Figure 8.2 records the typical 24 hours of Maya, a 38-year-old junior partner at a leading law firm, who defines her well-being and happiness in

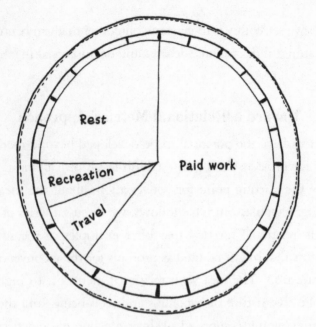

Figure 8.2: Maya's 24-hour Clock

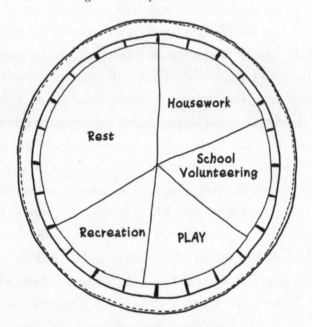

Figure 8.3: Josef's 24-hour Clock

terms of her career advancement and spends the bulk of her time focused on this paid work activity. In contrast, Josef is a 42-year-old sole parent living on a disability benefit who spends his typical day in a range of unpaid or alternatively paid work activities (see Figure 8.3). He carries out the housework associated with rearing his young family, spends time at the local school volunteering in the reading program, and puts energy into PLAY (an initiative he has started with other men in his neighbourhood who are also on disability or unemployment benefits to contribute to the neighbourhood by doing things such as helping single mums with tasks around their homes and building a community garden on vacant land). At the end of the day, he picks up his children from school and they spend time together doing the children's homework, reading and playing music.

WELL-BEING SCORECARD

MAYA'S WELL-BEING	1	2	3
Material			X
Occupational		X	
Social	X		
Community	X		
Physical		X	

Figure 8.4: Maya's Well-being Scorecard

Maya's and Josef's well-being are also gauged using a well-being scorecard on which they self-assess the five dimensions of well-being,[19] with scores of 1, 2 and 3 representing assessments of poor, sufficient and excellent (see Figures 8.4 and 8.5). Maya scores her material well-being as excellent, her occupational and physical well-being as sufficient, but her social and community well-being as poor. On the other hand, Josef assesses all dimensions of his well-being as excellent, except for his material well-being which he rates as sufficient.

WELL-BEING SCORECARD

JOSEF'S WELL-BEING	1	2	3
Material		X	
Occupational			X
Social			X
Community			X
Physical			X

Figure 8.5: Josef's Well-being Scorecard

Maya and Josef are clearly two extremes. One is oriented toward career advancement and material success; the other toward service to others and internal satisfaction. Most of us probably live some mix of these two. But the time-use clock and well-being scorecard can be used to open up discussions about how we achieve happiness and well-being. How do we spend the hours in a typical day? How do we assess the multiple dimensions of our well-being? To what extent do we prioritise paid work and material well-being as the means for achieving happiness, while potentially putting at risk other forms of well-being and eroding our chances of happiness, as Maya is doing? To what extent are we willing to follow Josef's path of moderating our material well-being in order to achieve happiness via the other dimensions of well-being?

The time-use clock and well-being scorecard are metrics that can be used to initiate an exploration of individual well-being and happiness. But what of the happiness and well-being of others and our planet? Here we can add another metric into the 'surviving well together' relationship. Today there are a plethora of ecological footprint calculators available online that allow us to measure the impact of how we live on the planet.[20] In Australia, the average ecological footprint is 3.7, meaning that Australians (on average) require 3.7 planets to sustain how we live.[21] Josef with his pared-down lifestyle can be sustained by 1.5 planets; whereas Maya, with her heavy reliance on consumption requires many more planets.[22] With the time-use clock, well-being scorecard and ecological footprint calculator it is possible to compare one's individual well-being with planetary well-being and ask, what is the ecological cost of my lifestyle? How does my work-life (im)balance relate to planetary sustainability? There are also relational metrics that can be used to interrogate how our attempts to achieve material well-being impact on others. The ethical interconnection checklist (see Table 8.1) invites us to consider what happens when we have to reach beyond our own capacity to meet our survival needs and use markets to provide what we need to survive well – the ethical interconnection checklist focuses our attention on what it means to survive well in relation to others. It asks us to consider how we are connected to those who supply our needs and to reflect on the impacts that our transactions have on others. It asks us to consider the well-being of animals, environments, workers and communities involved in supplying our needs, and it invites us to consider other ways that we might secure what we need to survive well.

Table 8.1: *The Ethical Interconnection Checklist*

ETHICAL INTERCONNECTION CHECKLIST		
THE ETHICAL CONCERN	THE ETHICAL QUESTIONS	THE PEOPLE AND PLANET CONNECTIONS
Are both my needs and the needs of others being met?	Am I connecting with others more directly? Am I taking only what I need? Are there other ways I can give back to help others meet their needs? Are there other ways I can share or reciprocate?	Animals Are animals being treated humanely? Environment Are the environmental impacts of production being addressed? People Is well-being taken into account? Politics Are the politics just? Sustainability Does the product have a neutral or positive impact?

Conclusion

In taking back the pursuit of happiness there is much to be done. Our attempts to place 'surviving well together' at the core of discussions about happiness can be seen as another way of applying the insights Bhutan offers the West. As the Prime Minister of Bhutan put it:

We have now clearly distinguished the 'happiness'…in GNH from the fleeting, pleasurable 'feel good' moods so often associated with that term. We know that true abiding happiness cannot exist while others suffer, and comes only from serving others, living in harmony with nature, and realising our innate wisdom and the true and brilliant nature of our own minds.[23]

Critically, we are not proposing another attempt to 'see like a survey' as John Law puts it,[24] although we acknowledge that some of the tools we are interested in (time-use surveys, well-being assessments, ecological footprint calculators and checklists) are also ones used to aggregate up to national happiness figures. Rather, we are imagining groups of people engaging in joint reflection on their lives as a prelude to collective actions to more effectively survive well together and in so doing achieve happiness. The exercise of interrogating different kinds of human and planetary happiness and using relational metrics in collective conversations has the potential to generate new economic possibilities. If we take back the economy as a site of ethical action, the pursuit of happiness becomes the pursuit of surviving well together. It becomes a means to develop greater capacity to connect and care. It prompts collective actions that promote global and local well-being. It generates new insights into the kinds of economy that might emerge if we are to take 'true abiding' human and planetary happiness seriously.

Endnotes

1   R. Easterlin, 'Does economic growth improve the human lot? Some empirical evidence', in P. A. David and M. W. Reder (eds), *Nations and Households in Economic Growth: Essays in Honor of Moses Abramovitz*, Academic Press, New York, 1974, pp. 89–125.

2   T. Jackson, *Prosperity without Growth: Economics for a Finite Planet*,
     Earthscan, London, 2009, pp. 39–43.

3   ibid., p. 40.

4   K. Ura, S. Alkire, T. Zangmo & K. Wangdi, *A Short Guide to Gross
     National Happiness Index*, Centre for Bhutan Studies, Thimpu, Bhutan,
     2012, p. 6.

5   In 2012, the Australia Bureau of Statistics identified 57 projects
     from across the globe aimed at interrogating societal well-being.
     These include projects at international, national and state levels.
     See Australian Bureau of Statistics, *Measures of Australia's Progress.
     Aspirations for our Nation: A Conversation with Australians about Progress*,
     Commonwealth of Australia, Canberra, 2012, p. 69.

6   Ura et al., *A Short Guide*, p. 1.

7   J. F. Helliwell, R. Layard & J. Sachs (eds), *World Happiness Report 2013*,
     UN Sustainable Development Solutions Network, New York, 2013,
     p. 66.

8   S. E. Merry, 'Measuring the world: indicators, human rights, and
     global governance', *Current Anthropology*, vol. 52, no. S3, 2011,
     pp. S83–S95.

9   ibid., p. S84.

10   ibid., p. S85.

11   J. Law, 'Seeing like a survey', *Cultural Sociology*, vol. 3, no. 2, 2009,
     pp. 239–56.

12   ibid., pp. 249–50.

13   This project is not unique in Australia. In line with Merry's work
     on measuring the world, by 2012 there were at least 51 indicator
     projects across Australia, run by national, state and local governments,
     examining concerns related to happiness and well-being. See
     Australian Bureau of Statistics, *Measures of Australia's Progress.
     Aspirations for our Nation: A Conversation with Australians about Progress*,
     Commonwealth of Australia, Canberra, 2012, p. 38.

14   Australian Bureau of Statistics, *Measures of Australia's Progress.
     Aspirations for our Nation: A Conversation with Australians about Progress*,
     Commonwealth of Australia, Canberra, 2012, p. 10.

15   ibid., p. 94.

16   ibid., p. 90.

17   ibid., p. 86.

18   The metrics discussed in this section are drawn from our recent
     book, J. K. Gibson-Graham, J. Cameron & S. Healy, *Take Back the*

Economy: An Ethical Guide for Transforming our Communities, University of Minnesota Press, Minneapolis, 2013.

19 Based on global research, Tom Rath and Jim Harter have identified five dimensions of well-being. Material well-being is having the resources to meet basic needs; occupational well-being is about enjoying what we do each day whether in paid, unpaid or alternatively paid work; social well-being is having close personal relationships; community well-being is being involved with community activities; and physical well-being is having good health and a safe living environment. See T. Rath & J. Harter, *Wellbeing: The Five Essential Elements*, Gallup Press, New York, 2010.

20 Two examples are the Global Footprint Network calculator (see http://www.footprintnetwork.org/en/index.php/gfn/page/calculators) and the World Wide Fund for Nature - Australia calculator (see http://www.wwf.org.au/our_work/people_and_the_environment/ human_footprint/footprint_calculator/).

21 Global Footprint Network, *The National Footprint Accounts, 2011 Edition*, Global Footprint Network, Oakland, California, 2012.

22 Gibson-Graham et al., *Take Back the Economy*, p. 34.

23 Cited in Ura et al., *A Short Guide*, p. 7.

24 Law, 'Seeing like a survey'.

#100HAPPYDAYS

James Arvanitakis

Characters in movies and on television are frequently asked, 'Are you happy?' Parents incessantly wish happiness upon their children: 'I just want them to be happy.' In her song *Just Be Happy*, pop singer Rihanna chants 'just as long as it makes you happy', over and over again.[1] Pharrel Williams in his international 2014 hit sings, 'Happy'. This search for happiness through love and partnership is also captured in the 2009 romantic comedy *He's Just Not That into You* when the Gigi character says:

> Girls are taught a lot of stuff growing up: if a boy punches you he likes you, never try to trim your own bangs, and someday you will meet a wonderful guy and get your very own happy ending. Every movie we see, every story we're told implores us to wait for it: the third act twist, the unexpected declaration of love, the exception to the rule.[2]

There are countless websites, self-help books and magazine articles on what makes us happy, often accompanied by a step-by-step guide. The lifestyle website *body+soul* lists 'Eight Steps to Happiness' beginning with 'Write your own eulogy'.[3] In

The Art of Happiness: A Guide to Developing Life's Most Important Skill Buddhist monk Matthieu Ricard observes that despite unprecedented prosperity, citizens in today's wealthy countries have never been more susceptible to depression and anxiety. The solution, according to Ricard, is

> twenty-minute exercises to train the mind to recog-
> nise and pursue happiness by concentrating on life's
> fundamentals, revealing the significant benefits that
> changing the way we view the world can bring to
> each of us.[4]

Also in the happiness and self-help genre is Sonja Lyubomirsky's step-by-step program, *The How of Happiness: A Scientific Approach to Getting the Life You Want*.[5] According to Lyubomirsky, each of us has a kind of happiness 'set point' which can be calibrated to different highs and lows. The book advises readers on how to raise this 'set point', find higher levels of happiness, and feel more satisfaction, more often. Motivational speaker Anthony Robbins also offers a great deal of advice on happiness. His books, websites, conferences and training programs, not to mention special appearances on Oprah Winfrey's *Life Class* series, tell us about the three steps we need to follow to find true happiness.[6] Indeed, Robbins has built a prosperous career linking happiness with success. His *Unleash the Power* training program is accompanied by testimonials from Bill Clinton and Hugh Jackman. Eight-time Grand Slam tennis champion André Agassi enthuses: 'Tony's incredible understanding of the world, people, and human nature makes him the ultimate life coach. He knows what it takes to make people...win!'[7]

In canvassing the mammoth volume of self-help literature, I find very little to salvage. One is left, at best, cynical, and at worst, feeling inadequate. This assessment is based on three broad observations. The first is that happiness is often identified as an 'end point': a place to which we travel. The second is focused on the individual and ignores any community bonds. In the words of Heidi Marie Rimke, this celebrates a culture of 'hyper-individuality for which an inherent, responsible relationality with others is actively discouraged and pathologised'.[8] Thirdly, it presents happiness as something that can be administered through a list of exercises, or checklists.[9]

Within this context, this chapter reflects on three inter-related questions. The first is to simply ask whether happiness is possible. Drawing on Sara Ahmed's 'feminist killjoys', I reflect on the fragility of happiness as the ultimate pursuit. The second is to consider alternatives to happiness. If, as indicated by the groaning shelves of self-help literature, happiness still eludes us, what alternatives are there to its 'pursuit'? Finally, I consider whether a social media experiment which promotes participation in a daily 'moments of happiness' may come closer to achieving what the self-help literature promises, but never achieves.

Is Happiness Possible?

The starting point of our journey is to ponder whether happiness is actually possible. If we accept that happiness is a state of being satisfied with one's life, at what point is it possible to say we are truly satisfied? Perhaps happiness relies on the way we view the world. Is happiness a function of the world around us or our own perception of it?

Can we be happy, for example, when successive Australian governments pursue brutal detention policies against refugees seeking asylum in this country, on our behalf, in our name? In this context, the pursuit of happiness can seem trivial or juvenile. By transporting asylum seekers, including children, across national borders from Australian detention centres to Papua New Guinea and Nauru, it has been said that the Australian government is itself involved in human trafficking.[10] Journalist and filmmaker John Pilger[11] and academic John Keane[12] have also controversially referred to these detention centres as 'concentration camps'.

Knowing that children are locked behind barbed wire, traumatised and ignored, would seem to make any sense of happiness experienced by the population for whose 'benefit' this is done empty and shallow. By a huge majority, asylum seekers who reach Australia are found to be refugees under international and Australian law. That is, these people are found to be fleeing persecution – war, conflict, tyranny – and yet we inflict further persecution in the form of indefinite detention in harsh and violent environments. These structures and practices are established and maintained by my government, ostensibly to protect the citizenship rights that people like me enjoy by an accident of birth.

In this picture, the pursuit of safety and freedom from persecution by asylum seekers is pitted against the happiness of the domestic population: two populations whose interests are said to be at odds. That is to say, the exclusion and brutal internment of refugees is justified on the grounds of national security – so the Australian population can feel safe – an element that we might consider key to a 'happy life'. Yet happiness of this sort requires the ability to ignore the plight of others.

Brutal policy on asylum seekers is not the only way government can and does operate against the happiness of many. Our record on 'internally displaced' persons, such as homeless people, is also dismal. Figures from Homelessness Australia indicate that on any single night, one person in every 200 experiences homelessness.[13] The principle cause of homelessness among women and children is male violence: two-thirds of homeless children are accompanying a woman escaping domestic violence.[14] Other reasons range from entrenched, structural inequality; inadequate affordable housing supply; intergenerational poverty; and long-term unemployment. In a wealthy nation of only 23 million people, this figure ought to be astonishing. But the policies which produce it, including outsourcing to organisations with very long records of neglect and abuse, continue to be pursued. This means the situation will not turn around in the short term. In this context, is pursuing happiness possible – or even desirable? Can I feel happy when, within metres of my comfortable, warm home, secured by the wealth that self-help ideologies insist that I deserve,[15] people are sleeping on the streets and scavenging for food in bins outside the door?

Feminist Killjoys

Sara Ahmed takes a similar journey in questioning the pursuit of happiness in her well-recognised work 'Feminist Killjoys',[16] which was promptly followed by her book, *The Promise of Happiness*. In these texts, Ahmed undertakes a robust cultural analysis of the idea of 'happiness' as it functions in present day Britain – but with much broader relevance.[17] It is worth recounting Ahmed's arguments, as she simultaneously captures the individualised nature of happiness that allows us to ignore the plight of others, and the idea that happiness is something that *someone else* can bestow upon you. Happiness, Ahmed argues, is that which we 'promise to give to others as an expression of love'. We say, 'I just want you to be happy'.

This speech act of desiring someone 'to be happy', according to Ahmed, appears as an offer of freedom: do what you want, whatever it is that will make you happy. Yet on closer inspection, the statement may be more akin to a command. It requires the other person to do what is expected of them, to undertake actions which will lead to some kind of 'happiness' end point. In this way, 'I want you to be happy' really means 'I want you to do what I think makes you happy'.

Hence, such innocent sounding phrases such as 'I just want you to be happy' or 'I'm happy if you're happy' are caught up in complicated kinds of power relationships. They create a demand, or instruction, to perform a kind of 'happiness duty'. This sets up an expectation that happiness will follow if we participate in what is judged 'good', and if we live our lives in the 'right' way. In short, the implied freedom promised by the pursuit of happiness is limited. It directs us away from one set of life choices to another. In illustrating these cultural dynamics, Ahmed draws on a rich array of books, films and television shows where the most common narrative direction is towards oppressive and even unobtainable social norms such as 'whiteness' and 'heterosexuality'. In *Bend it Like Beckham* (directed by Gurinder Chadha), for example, the character Jess must choose between spending time with her Indian Sikh migrant family, or playing football with her white heterosexual friends. In Nancy Garden's *Annie on My Mind*, the parents may not be unhappy about a child 'coming out' as same-sex attracted, but they are unhappy that their child will be unhappy because of the 'challenges' of homophobia that will follow.

Ahmed is not against happiness – that would be like railing against motherhood, or peace (though that is certainly possible). Rather, her ultimate focus is the moral order imposed on the commanded by the directive to 'just be happy'. Those who refuse to participate in this moral order, according to Ahmed, are labelled 'killjoys' – the humourless feminist, the bitchy queer, the angry young black person or the melancholy migrant. These are the guests at the dinner party who remind us of the plight of refugees, or the fact that our privilege exists at the expense and exclusion of others. The killjoy may be anyone who does not pursue individualised forms of happiness.

Hope and Happiness

What is the alternative to this pursuit of happiness which we find in the self-help literature that Ahmed deconstructs so successfully? One possibility, I would argue, is 'hope'.

Before proceeding, a little background. Early in my research career, I was struck with a question: whenever we study conflict, we turn to the various socio-cultural reasons that lead to war, but rarely analyse what leads a war-torn community to peace. Certainly, we can look at decisive victories and understand that one side was left with little choice, but when fractured communities start to rebuild we are left merely puzzled.

Having worked in a number of conflict and postconflict zones, I began looking for a common thread that led to the rebuilding of communities, drawing particularly on the research of Ghassan Hage.[18] Hope, according to Hage, does not emerge sitting at home waiting for things to get better. Hope is an active process, and requires agency. Hope is both having a sense that a better world is possible *as well as* a sense of agency, a capacity to contribute to this 'bettering'. These elements, when combined, engage and empower the individual. Hope must be active and productive – a better world achieved through actions.[19]

The key is forging a connection between individual and societal hope. Social happiness does not exist at the cost of individual happiness: it expands the desire for happiness as a whole. Individual hope combined with societal hope, the vision of a better world, and the actions that bring about change, can expand hope to include those experiencing despair.

Henry A. Giroux echoes these sentiments, claiming the 'pursuit of happiness and the good life is a collective affair'.[20] Giroux links this pursuit of happiness with a sense of hope, which he argues is but one ingredient required for a more just world. Other ingredients are 'reason, imagination, and moral responsibility'. This link is important because Giroux draws a line between public challenges and individual and collective pursuits of hope and happiness. Further, both Giroux and Hage make the point that the individual is never separate from the collective, and as such, nor is the aspiration for hope and happiness.

Pursuing Happiness

Does this mean that we should discount happiness altogether? My critique here is not of the pursuit of happiness per se. Rather, I seek to take on the dominant construction of happiness as an individualised affair with a standard checklist and a certain end point. These messages are loud and clear and adopted by many, but they are simple and selfish too. Given that the next generation often absorbs the dominant message, it is critical for academics and other teachers to be attuned to what they are hearing and to counter dangerously misleading claims. When teaching the next generation (and our own children), it is imperative to reach out, to invite participation, and to contextualise experiences in a way that is relevant, including to the most vulnerable.

One recent example is the social media experiment, '100HappyDays'. The website 100HappyDays.com was launched on 30 December 2013,[21] together with a social media campaign branded under the hashtag #100HappyDays. It challenges participants to collect 100 happy moments over 100 days and take a photo of the specific instant. The point, according to the website, is to 'remind you about the beauty of your life'. Since its inception, I have been fascinated by this project because it directs people to focus on the small, mundane and random moments that can bring happiness – every day. According to the website, 100HappyDays is *not*:

> …a happiness competition or a showing off contest. If you try to please/make others jealous via your pictures – you lose without even starting. Same goes for cheating.

It does not appear to attract people who post photos of their shopping sprees, or recently acquired gadgets, or engage in extreme events, as so many 'boast posts' do. Rather, there are photos of flowers, friends, pets, food and local neighbourhoods:

moments often shared and frequently unplanned.[22] It is everyday happiness that captures the imagination and interest here. In a digital age of smartphone-enabled constant connection and sharing, the capturing of these moments performs a kind of re-enchantment of the world.

Amidst the plethora of self-help guides and books that outline the steps to happiness, fulfilment, or, more often, 'winning' and 'success', the idea of 'instagram' appreciation in the everyday, I would argue, has three important consequences. Firstly, it directs us to re-engage with the immediate reality around us rather than look for excitement elsewhere. We all enjoy a holiday, but such times represent only a small fraction of life experience. Holidays are relatively expensive and when we return, our lives tend to go back to the same patterns. Secondly, the focus on the everyday is a focus on our cultural practices, on the things that we do, which stimulate our enjoyment. Thirdly, #100HappyDays inspires moments of reflection. In the contemporary world, an instant of boredom is routinely filled, and thus moments of reflection become rare. The #100HappyDays challenge directs us to reflect, and thus to reflective moments. It is in the everyday that people take time to identify these moments, not in what Ahmed describes as the societal pursuit framed by dominant cultures.

The #100HappyDays challenge does not end the plight of refugees or house the homeless. What it does do, however, is challenge the individualised nature of happiness as described by self-help literature. It highlights that our own pursuit of happiness does not have to come at the expense of others. There is a 'do no harm' characteristic element to this type of happiness.

Our everyday cultural practices can point to a broader cultural shift. And it is here that we may we find moments of hope to confront exclusion and displacement.

Of course, not everyone is convinced that there are tangible benefits. According to the site itself, 71 per cent of people have not reached the 100-day goal 'quoting lack of time as the main reason'.[23] Commenting on the project in mainstream media, Jamie Gruman raised the concern that 100 consecutive happy days are not possible, and its pursuit could have the opposite effect.[24] Such concerns are certainly valid, but I would argue that the challenge does not set out to force people to be happy, or to appear happy. It prompts participants to actively seek out moments of happiness in daily interactions and experiences, and take a moment to reflect and appreciate such instances. It echoes Eleanor Roosevelt's valuable advice that happiness is a by-product of experiences, not an end in itself.[25]

Unleashing Happiness

Hope, I have argued elsewhere, is like Norman Lindsey's magic pudding: the more you share, the larger it grows, and the greater its value.[26] Hope is the antithesis of a commodity where scarcity drives the value. Hage, for example, describes a society with declining hope as a 'shrinking society'. We can think of hope as a cultural commons, something that is fundamental to ensuring we live in an authentic community, rather than as a group of individuals in close proximity. But it is, of course, essential to draw links between the hope and agency of individuals and that of society.

The test for #100HappyDays, and other cultural innovations, is to make this link between the individual and the social, including where the individual–social relationship is established via digital or social media. This is not just the alternative understanding of cultural studies and sociologist scholars. It is confirmed by 'happiness economics', groups of psychologists and economists who, among other findings, note that 'the best way to predict how much we will enjoy an experience is not to evaluate its characteristics ourselves, but to see how much other people liked it'.[27]

Moments of reflection and enchantment are fundamental to our ongoing search for fulfilment and purpose, but we must ensure that we forge and strengthen links between these moments of happiness and the pursuit of a just world that is accountable to the displaced, excluded, vulnerable and persecuted. Anything less than the twin goals of individual and societal happiness necessarily leave us empty – and it is here the self-help literature is at its emptiest. Neither goal guarantees 'happiness', nor should we see either goal as an end point. Combined, they offer the by-product of happiness. It is a by-product worth reflecting on.

Endnotes

1   S. Smith, M. J. Sparkman & M. D. Allen, *Just be Happy*, Emi April Music Publishing, New York, 2006.

2   G. Behrendt & L. Tuccillo with A. Kohn & M. Silverstein, *He's Just Not That Into You*, New Line Cinema Corporation and Flower Films, New York, 2009.

3   A. Grant & A. Leigh, *Eight Steps to Happiness*, http://www.bodyandsoul.com.au/sex+relationships/wellbeing/eight+steps+to+happiness,6693, viewed 23 February 2014.

4   M. Ricard, *The Art of Happiness: A Guide to Developing Life's Most Important Skill*, Little, Brown, Paris, 2011.

5   S. Lyubomirsky, *The How of Happiness: A scientific approach to getting the life you want*, Penguin Press, New York, 2008.

6   A. Robbins, *Success Secrets: Things You Need To Make It To The Top*, Oprah Winfrey Network via The Huffington Post, 2013, http://www.huffingtonpost.com/2013/01/28/tony-robbins-success-secrets-make-it_n_2553113.html, viewed 23 February 2014.

7   A. Robbins, *5 Keys to Break Through Stress*, UPW, 2014, http://www.unleashthepowerwithinaustralia.com/?gclid=CMjLhOyk3L0CFRdwv AodkhcARA, viewed 23 February 2014.

8   H. M. Rimke, 'Governing citizens through self-help literature', *Cultural Studies*, vol. 14, no. 1, 2000, pp. 61–78.

9   B. Hamstra, *Why Good People Do Bad Things*, Carol Publishing Group, New York, 1996.

10 L. Briskman & C. Goddard, 'Australia trafficks and abuses asylum seeker children', Melbourne, *Age*, 25 February 2014, http://www.theage.com.au/comment/australia-trafficks-and-abuses-asylum-seeker-children-20140224-33cxs.html#ixzz2yjZ6KMBe, viewed 25 February 2014.

11 J. Pilger, 'No shipload of whites fleeing disaster would be treated like this', Sydney, *Sydney Morning Herald*, 6 November 2009, http://www.smh.com.au/federal-politics/society-and-culture/no-shipload-of-whites-fleeing-disaster-would-be-treated-like-this-20091105-i067.html#ixzz32OIphAXj, viewed 15 May 2014.

12 J. Keane, 'When concentration camps and democracy clash', Sydney, *ABC The Drum*, 28 April 2014, http://www.abc.net.au/news/2014-04-28/keane-when-concentration-camps-and-democracy-clash/5397152, viewed 15 May 2014.

13 Homelessness Australia, *Homelessness in Australia*, Fact Sheet, 2011–12, http://www.homelessnessaustralia.org.au/images/publications/Fact_Sheets/Homelessness_in_Australia_v2.pdf.

14 Homelessness Australia, *Homelessness and Women*, Fact Sheet, 2011–12, http://www.homelessnessaustralia.org.au/UserFiles/File/Fact%20sheets/Fact%20Sheets%202011-12/Homelessness%20&%20Women%202011-12(8).pdf, viewed 23 February 2014.

15 P. Mccoll, *21 Distinctions of Wealth: Attract the Abundance You Deserve*, Hay House, California, 2008.

16 S. Ahmed, 'Feminist Killjoys (And Other Willful Subjects)', *The Scholar and Feminist Online*, issue 8, no.3, 2010, http://sfonline.barnard.edu/polyphonic/print_ahmed.htm, viewed 23 February 2014.

17 S. Ahmed, *The Promise of Happiness*, Duke University Press, Durham, NC, 2010.

18 G. Hage, *Against Paranoid Nationalism: Searching for Hope in a Shrinking Society*, Pluto Press, Sydney, 2003.

19 J. Arvanitakis, *The Cultural Commons of Hope: The Attempt to Commodify the Final Frontier of the Human Experience*, Verlag, Berlin & New York, 2007.

20 H. A. Giroux, *Translating the Future and the Promise of Democracy*, Convocation Address, Memorial University, Newfoundland CA, 2005, http://www.henryagiroux.com/awards/convocation_address.htm, viewed 24 February 2014.

21 100HappyDays.com

22 Huffpost Healthy Living, 'This Is What 100 Days Of Happiness Looks Like', 20 March 2014, http://www.huffingtonpost.com/2014/03/20/100-happy-days_n_4995007.html, viewed 21 March 2014.

23 100HappyDays.com

24 R. O'Flanagan, 'Local professor rains on 100 Days of Happiness Movement', *Guelph Mercury*, Ontario, 21 March 2014, http://www.guelphmercury.com/news-story/4437771-local-professor-rains-on-100-days-of-happiness-movement/, viewed 22 March 2014; see also CBC News, 'Happiness challenge may lead to sadness, psychologist warns', 26 March 2014, http://www.cbc.ca/news/health/happiness-challenge-may-lead-to-sadness-psychologist-warns-1.2587675, viewed 27 March 2014.

25 E. Roosevelt, *You Learn by Living: Eleven Keys for a More Fulfilling Life*, Westminster John Knox Press, Louisville KY, 1960, p. 95.

26 Arvanitakis, *Cultural Commons*.

27 R. Gittens, *How to get more Happiness per Dollar*, 18 June 2014, http://www.rossgittins.com/2014/06/how-to-get-more-happiness-per-dollar.html, viewed 20 June 2014.

'STOP LAUGHING – THIS IS SERIOUS': THE 'LARRIKIN CARNIVALESQUE' IN AUSTRALIA

Tony Moore

The problem with contemporary ideas about happiness is their intolerance of personal and social discontent. Western societies have moved from the enlightenment idea of the 'pursuit of happiness' as a utilitarian measure of a healthy, democratic body politic to a new-age discourse of self-help, positive thinking, and management-imposed workplace 'wellness'.[1] Happiness has morphed into a personal responsibility to avoid negative, critical responses to the external conditions of our lives, lest we court depression, anxiety or disturb the tranquillity and happiness of others. If we are unhappy, the problem lies with us, and not our job, family situation, neighbourhood or rulers. In this individualised but mass-marketed therapeutic iteration, happiness is too often construed as a form of quiescence, of contentment, acceptance of social norms and conformity to the status quo. This coercive species of happiness is not new, and had echoes in twentieth-century corporate management practice, communist and fascist social engineering, and utopian town planning, and as an ideology percolated through a myriad of mid-twentieth-century American family television programs promoting ideal, middle-class family life in a free-enterprise society. This type of mandated and homogeneous happiness is coercive, the enemy of creativity, freedom, pluralism and genuine human feeling.

In this chapter I want to draw the idea of happiness away from passivity and surrender to the existing social order, and recast it as a form of carnival: a subversive, rambunctious style of happiness derived from transgressive art and 'art of the self'; a comedic disruption to conformity that destabilises complacent authority, producing new ways of seeing and being. Sara Ahmed, drawing on feminist, black and queer studies, has demonstrated how happiness has been used to justify oppression and social conformity. But where Ahmed critiques the happiness police by examining the 'raging revolutionaries' who deploy a kind of unhappiness to promote social progress, my interest is with radicals who use happiness as a form of liberation.[2]

Surveying Australian political culture, the historian Manning Clark warned of the 'straighteners', the puritanical punishers who came not just from the right, but also from well-meaning radicals and reformers on the left. The new societies these grim radicals hope to build may not turn out to be happy for most of us. Too often when political radicals of the left or right seek to expose society's ills and promote reform or revolution they revel in holier-than-thou virtue, righteous anger or a superior kind of charity. John Pilger, for example, performs a valuable service using the documentary form to reveal terrible, systematic oppression, exploitation, even genocide – causes of profound unhappiness in the world – but is not known for leavening his polemics with life-affirming humour. Indeed, writing in the *New Statesmen* about the plight of indigenous Australians he wondered how scholars like myself could defend an 'Australian patriotism based on taking the piss, on laughing, not just at oneself but at the powerful', and advised 'until we Whites give back to Black Australians their nationhood, we can never claim our own'.[3] But what of the role of satire and humour as a way of commenting on, and indeed changing society? Means shape ends and, to channel American socialist Emma Goldman, if you can't laugh I don't want to be part of your revolution. It is my contention that in Australia from its beginnings, humour, irony, the send-up has been one small weapon in the armoury of the oppressed, the outcast, or those simply fed up with cultural uniformity. This fightback begins with Aboriginal people who, as Larissa Behrendt argues in another essay in this volume, have long used wry and ironic humour against authorities as a form of resistance to colonisation. Indeed Australia's sense of humour may well owe more to its original inhabitants than to the undoubted anti-authoritarian mockery of the convicts and the early colonies' cockney and Celtic immigrants – many of whom were also victims of dispossession in the Old World, seeking happiness in the New.

These early influences shape an Australian style of cultural subversion that I call the 'Larrikin Carnivalesque'.[4] It is where rabble-rousing lefties meet a style of libertarianism that can also be associated with right-leaning contrarians. It has a long pedigree in the arts, stretching from groups of bohemian writers, journalists and cartoonists gathered around the early *Bulletin* in the late nineteenth century, to *Kath and Kim* and prankster John Safran in this century. For me, this home-grown comedic tradition had its climax in the Fosters-guzzling, all-chundering Barry McKenzie movies of the early 1970s, but it stretches back deep into colonial Australia, and is alive and vulgar in the contemporary Australia of *The Chaser*, *Jonah from Tonga* and *Housos*.

The term 'Carnivalesque' was coined by Soviet literary academic Mikhail Bakhtin to refer to a topsy-turvy spirit of riotous festivity, famously unleashed in the carnivals of Europe in the fifteenth and sixteenth centuries, in which the lower orders deployed misrule, play, humour and vulgarity to subvert authority – if only temporarily.[5] The Carnivalesque was a way of conceptualising a style of dissent that was evident in the literature of Rabelais, and stretched back to the ritualised chaos of the Roman Saturnalia. In such revels and festivals, vulgarity was deployed to profane the sacred and bring down to earth the mighty and pious. Bakhtin rightly perceived the subversive power of spectacle and festivity, and elements of misrule such as drunkenness, gluttony, parody, sexual ribaldry, gender confusion, gender bending, riot, the grotesque, and combining the sacred and profane.[6] By crossing arbitrary borders and disrupting expectation, carnival could stimulate new ways of thinking and radically transform culture. While it was more of a safety valve than a revolution, Bakhtin argued that carnival nevertheless had the potential to make the rulers squirm with discomfort by ridiculing the mystique of power and by overturning customary hierarchies. He must have been on to something because Stalin exiled him to Kazakhstan.

The intellectuals of the midcentury Sydney Libertarian 'Push' created an Australian variant. Influenced by John Anderson, these critical thinkers and drinkers argued that utopias of the left and right were authoritarian illusions, and that freedom is achieved in the act of contestation, by permanent protest against governing orthodoxies, and by a nonconformist, libertine lifestyle that delivered personal escape from servility to the state, the market and the homogeneous 'quietism' of Australian suburban domesticity. The Libertarians opposed notions such as the 'common good', of correct ways, perceiving society as pluralist, where different interests were in conflict. Translated to the classic liberal idea of the pursuit of happiness, it can be argued that in an unequal society, happiness is not equally distributed, and some people's happiness is achieved at the cost of another's unhappiness, even misery. In this circumstance of happiness inequality, carnival is something of a fightback, where those unhappy about this uneven distribution temporarily turn the tables, enjoying some happiness at the expense of those who benefit from the status quo.

Carnivalesque dissent has deep roots in Australia's folk memory where it's often referred to as our 'larrikin streak'. The original larrikins were working class, sometimes Irish, delinquent youths who gathered in gangs called 'pushes', and disturbed the peace of city streets from the 1870s into the early decades of the twentieth century.[7] Their cocky sense of entitlement and disregard for class hierarchy surprised and shocked. While becoming the focus of a conservative moral panic, larrikinism also came to be admired by artistic libertines from the 1890s as a marker for nonconformity, earthy humour and disdain for authority. Where nineteenth-century Parisian writers such as Henry Murger or Hugo had romanticised that city's *bohémiens*, or gypsies, as markers of freedom and spontaneity, many Australian writers identified with the larrikins' unruly, disrespectful, somewhat threatening behaviour. In what follows I consider key moments of the Carnivalesque in our cultural and political life, debunking the myth of the earnest, angry zealot (so often the architects of mass unhappiness in their virtuous intolerance of heresy, imperfection and fun), and celebrate the life-affirming role of humour, satire, irony and play, disrupting conventional ideas about the pursuit of social happiness.

The Colonial Carnivalesque

One of Australia's great colonial satirists was journalist and writer Marcus Clarke.[8] Before digging into the archives, I had imagined the author of *For the Term of His Natural Life* to be a crusty venerable Victorian, but discovered a wild child inspired by the ironies of a strange new society, who penned his gothic classic at only twenty-five! A celebrated wit, he drank, argued and scandalised his way through Melbourne in the 1870s, setting up a string of bohemian clubs, outraging respectable society, and trying to keep one step ahead of the creditors. Clarke came to prominence in his early twenties as a columnist in the politically conservative yet culturally sophisticated news-paper the *Argus*. Scalpel in one hand and rapier in the other, young Marcus carved out a journalistic niche for himself as the 'Peripatetic Philosopher', a slightly bemused, cynical observer of the (mock) heroic goings on of Melbourne society, producing sketches that anticipate Humphries's character monologues a century later. His topical, blasé style resonated with the young city's humour. His targets included the 'Parochial Committee Man' – 'bland, pious' and 'solemn-looking', 'intensely respect-able, and intensely narrowminded' – who dominated politics of the period. He had little time for zealous radicals either. He condemned colonial republicans as 'kid glove democrats' who 'profess to admire Cromwell…talk about liberty of the soul, equality of honest men, but would disdain to nod to their tailor if they met him in the street'. Few were exempt from his barbs, including sharebrokers, 'new chums', 'our boys', the working man, politicians, squatters, art connoisseurs, journalists, sport-ing men, ladies and larrikins, all accompanied by their own peculiar slang or jargon.[9]

A punk in the age of steam, Clarke's writing became increasingly transgressive. He caused an international stir with a syndicated joke column purporting to expose an order of orgiastic Carmelite nuns in Melbourne. He anticipated television by contriving a hoax that images of the Melbourne Cup were transmitted into the offices of the *Herald* by means of a great optical eye suspended in the sky.[10] In a mock pamphlet *The Future Australian Race*, sending up fashionable racial theories, he predicted that by 1977 Queensland and all 'hot' areas above a certain line would be authoritarian potentates like those found in Latin America and the Orient, while the south will be a Greek democracy: 'The intellectual capital of this Republic will be Victoria'. However 'the fashionable and luxurious capital' will be 'on the shore of Sydney Harbour'. 'The present custom of drinking alcohol to excess…will continue,' he concluded.[11] He told the readers of the *Argus*, 'I like to see human life with its coat off, and to descend an octave on the social scale'.[12] He despised the colonial materialism promoted by a ruling class of jumped up 'businessmen', and became an unlikely crusader for the poor, for Tasmanian Aboriginals, for liberal secular humanism, and most famously, convicts. Ultimately the wayward author picked one fight too many and was frozen out by the Melbourne establishment and fell far and hard. In crossing the class and other boundaries, such as solvency and sobriety, which distinguished the respectable, the bohemianism of Clarke became offensive to a new society still insecure about its origins. Marcus Clarke died prematurely, a bankrupt at age thirty-five in 1881.

Nevertheless, the seeds of bohemian social happiness sown by Clarke and his circle took off like Paterson's Curse among the

Australian-born of the next generation. At the *Bulletin* magazine, founded in 1880, this radical, democratic, grassroots Australian Carnivalesque humour continued to flourish.[13] Its early editor J. F. Archibald made a virtue of tapping the energies of bush and urban workers, the shearing sheds and city pubs, and from this interactive community emerged writers with a gift for the vernacular as diverse as Henry Lawson, C. J. Dennis, Miles Franklin, Steele Rudd, Banjo Patterson, Joseph Furphy and the cartoonist Norman Lindsay. The *Bulletin* drew on the language of the streets and the shearing sheds to mock those in authority, from the capitalist 'fat man', 'squatters', parsons, 'wowsers' and magistrates to plutocrats, governors and the Crown. A particular target was the 'wowser', slang for a pious, Christian proselytiser of either gender who was vigilant in policing others' morals, skilled in the tut-tutting of others' happiness. Notwithstanding a nasty strain of sexism and racism in its humour, the *Bulletin* was radical in its championing of causes such as one man one vote, republicanism, unions, the new Labor Party and female suffrage. But as Sylvia Lawson has argued, it was in the magazine's disruption of expectation – its topsy-turvy mockery of authority, the blending of genres, the interplay of short comic pars with cartoons – that the *Bulletin* was most subversive, helping to create a cultural blooming distinguished by its appeal to both the salon and the saloon.[14]

Thoroughly Modern Carnival

While the qualities of larrikinism, mateship and knock-about bush egalitarianism romanticised by the *Bulletin* were conscripted into imperial service in World War I, and shorn of their radicalism as part of the 'Anzac Legend', a modern, more female-friendly and sexually libertine version of the Carnivalesque burst into fluorescence in jazz-age Sydney. The new centre for playful journalism was *Smith's Weekly*, which reporter Elizabeth Riddel claimed 'cut the powerful down to size, and crusaded for the battler'. 'It had a knock down, drag out policy of let's be rude to everything'.[15] At the 1923 Sydney Artists' Ball, romance writer and journalist Dulcie Deamer acquired instant notoriety by wearing a skimpy leopard-skin minidress and a dog-tooth necklace, and was crowned 'Queen of Bohemia'. Like Sydney's Gay and Lesbian Mardis Gras at the end of the twentieth century, the Artists' Balls of the Roaring Twenties were a steamy stage on which to exhibit new freedoms. While police tried to suppress these parties, Deamer could happily report that 'a glittering flood was threatening the dike that dammed it, and those in uniform...lost the battle.'[16] World War I had loosened many nineteenth-century restrictions on women and some, like the talented and feisty Dulcie, were welcomed as journalists and became leading exponents of the Larrikin Carnivalesque – in her case, presiding as the 'Grand Initiator' at the Noble Order of I Felici, Literati, Cognoscenti e Lunatici – the Happy, Literary, Wise and Mad.[17] A lasting symbol of Australia's interwar modern urban comedy is the *Smith's Weekly* cartoon by Stan Cross of two guffawing workmen dangling off a skyscraper girder, one hanging precariously onto the other's trousers, which have fallen down. It is captioned: 'For gor'sake stop laughing, this is serious'.

The notorious Ern Malley hoax of 1944 built on Sydney bohemia's love of japes and stunts, and was a perfectly executed satire of the serious young zealots of the burgeoning modernist movement in Melbourne and Adelaide, focused on the *Angry*

Penguins journal.[18] In April 1944, Penguin-in-chief Max Harris received a manuscript of unpublished surrealist poems penned by an unheard-of poet and mechanic, named Ern Malley, who had recently died and left his oeuvre for his sister, Ethel, to find. Convinced they had discovered an Australian T. S. Eliot, Harris and patron John Reed published the poems in *Angry Penguins* magazine to great fanfare, appearing simultaneously in Melbourne and New York, replete with a cover showing a painting of Malley by Sidney Nolan. But a few months later the poems were revealed to be a hoax, concocted by two solider poets from Sydney, James McAuley and Harold Stewart, supposedly in an afternoon at Victoria Barracks. They told the press '[w]e opened books at random, choosing a word or phrase haphazardly. We made lists of these and wove them into nonsensical sentences.' Their literary purpose was to expose what they considered the lack of standards within an emerging Australian avant-garde desperate to catch up with a Europe 'who fell for humourless nonsense'.[19] McAuley and Stewart were fine poets, and their mock modernism can today be appreciated as unintentional stream-of-consciousness masterpieces. As noted by Robert Hughes, their invention of the prim and philistine Ethel Malley anticipated Edna Everage by a decade.

Indeed, by the 1950s Barry Humphries was already disturbing the peace, using Dadaist pranks to upset Melbourne's postwar 'niceness' and to misanthropically expose the foibles of human nature. As a young performance artist he would eat fake vomit off the street with a spoon, or pretend to beat a hapless blind man on a tram (the blind man played by another actor) just to observe people's reactions, to disrupt the Brack-like commuter trance. Humphries honed his writing and acting skills satirising the suburban middle and working classes. Edna Everage, Humphries's revenge on the smug and philistine suburban middle class, first appeared in a TV sketch in 1956 as an Olympic hostess, driving an official to apoplexy as she primly rejected all nationalities offered as billets for her Moonee Ponds home. But by 1965 the left and arts types were also in his sights.

The postwar expansion of universities provided a stage for young bohemians such as Humphries, Germaine Greer, Clive James and Bob Ellis to hone the larrikin Carnivalesque, literally in student revue, and also in campus newspapers such as *Honi Soit* and *Tharunka*, where Richard Neville, Martin Sharpe and Richard Walsh rehearsed a new wave of libertarian satire that went off-campus as *Oz*. In 1964 *Oz* magazine landed like a meteorite into what its young editors derided as the complacent Australian media landscape. It was amusingly critical of the institutions that spoke for a conservative idea of nation, such as state and federal governments, the courts, police and army, the RSL and service clubs. Satire, absurdity, sex and vulgarity marked the magazine out from the broadsheets and worthy avant-garde publications, and had more in common with university revues. Neville's *Play Power* published in 1971 makes it clear that his brand of countercultural satire was not just hostile to the right, but also to the left, for being too elitist in its politics and too dismissive of the revolutionary possibilities of pop culture, humour and media. This strategy was the modus operandi of *Oz*, but also other counter cultural periodicals such as the off-campus anticensorship *Thorunka*, where student editor Wendy Bacon turned up to the paper's obscenity trial in 1970 dressed as a nun and bearing a sign reading, 'I've been fucked by God's steel prick'. Germaine Greer's *The Female Eunuch* advocated 'delinquency' and sexual pleasure among women as the path to female empowerment.[20] This new politics was essentially Carnivalesque: decentralising power, popular, pluralist and using unruliness, obscenity, vulgarity and humour against the centralised power of traditional bourgeois and socialist politics. Unsurprisingly it was advanced by minority and social movements locked out of mainstream power, not least the militant 'black power' phase in the long Aboriginal struggle for decolonisation and land rights, dramatically symbolised by the erection on Australia Day 1972 of the Aboriginal Tent Embassy, outside Parliament House in Canberra – both a radical political act and a supreme moment of political theatre.[21]

The Contemporary Carnivalesque

I grew up in working-class Port Kembla and Dapto in the 1970s, where we cheered on Bazza McKenzie, the gormless young Australian larrikin in London, brainchild of Barry Humphries, collaborating with director Bruce Beresford and producer Phillip Adams, who seemed to catch an emerging mood. Self-described as an ordinary 'working man', Bazza was one of us, a life-affirming foil against smug trendies, snivelling officials, puffing pollies and the xenophobic of all classes.[22] He was vulgar and irrepressible, perpetually sucking on 'ice cold tubes of Fosters', trying unsuccessfully to get 'a sheila into a game of sink the sausage', and 'chundering' at will on unfortunate 'poms', trendies and countercultural 'ratbags' who crossed his inebriated path. McKenzie is badged as a relic from a bygone era by his double-breasted suit and especially his hat, and set lose amongst the hustlers, artists, hippies, ad men, immigrants and women's libbers that made up the changing world. However, the ocker trend was criticised by an older generation of Australian sophisticates who were too distracted by the vulgarity and suburban audiences mouthing Bazza's colourful slang to notice the satire of an Australian society in flux.

The people behind these popular cultural phenomena were far from mere commercial showmen, and they smuggled into them all sorts of critical insights and visceral pleasures from bohemian subcultures such as the Sydney 'Push' and the Melbourne 'Drift' of the 1950s, and the experimental avant-garde projects at which they laboured in the 1960s. The ockers of stage and screen interrogated key tensions in our culture at the time – between provincial Australia and the British metropolitan centre, the artist and the working class, the wowser and the libertine, authority and unruliness, cosmopolitanism and white Australia. Bob Ellis chimed in that '[a] country can't mature until it has learned to celebrate its gaucheries.'[23] This sense of self-satire was epitomised in the 1974 sequel *Barry McKenzie Holds His Own*, famously climaxing in a cameo by Prime Minister Gough Whitlam, where he regally 'dames' Bazza's Aunty Edna Everage. The scene recalls a colourful period when the Larrikin Carnivalesque moved to the centre of our political culture, an era in which leaders laughed along with us at our foibles, engendering a healthy national happiness. Not for nothing did Whitlam once observe 'the fun is where I am'.

Today faction-controlled preselections sift out the colourful, the larrikin, the eccentrics for the party hacks and machine men on both sides of parliament. Dulling down our politics with their technocratic jargon, spin and cronyism, these sawdust

Machiavellis have sapped some of the happiness out of our public life, evident in the disillusionment of Australians with their current leaders, and the embrace of colourful, eccentric independents from outside the mainstream. We live in an age where bureaucrats are drafted as politicians, where managerialism, focus groups and gaffe-spotting take the place of wit, passion and ideas. But perhaps because of this political tedium, the Larrikin Carnivalesque has thrived in recent decades, with the ear for accent and social nuance passing to new generations. The Anglo-Celts lost their monopoly on larrikinism in the 1990s as 'wog humour' emerged from the suburbs with another popular movie where the naïve but vulgar innocent triumphs in Nick Giannopoulos's *Wog Boy*. Kath and Kim have confirmed Edna's secret that women indeed rule the childlike men of the suburbs, and they now do so not by shushing male pleasures but by out-ockering them. Paul Fennech's *Pizza* franchise and its latest iteration, *Housos*, has the happy power to offend and shock while empowering those on society's margins. But through the long haul of the Howard, Rudd, Gillard and now Abbott years it has been The Chaser team who today channel the subversive elements of the Larrikin Carnivalesque – anarchic antiauthoritarianism, pranks, the parody of other media, and flirtation with obscenity and offences against good taste. Like Humphries and *Oz*, The Chaser are interested in the abuse of power and hypocrisy wherever they lurk: in corporations, public service, the media, celebrity culture, religion, unions. The Chaser team has been pilloried by the great and worthy, but not as yet imprisoned. They came close, though, with an inspired stunt during the APEC summit in Sydney in 2007, driving a black limo carrying Chas Licciardello (dressed as Osama bin Laden) effortlessly through check points.

Humphries's gift for dark, ironic social observations has now passed to Chris Lilley, whose *We Can Be Heroes, Summer Heights High, Angry Boys, Jamie* and *Jonah from Tonga* dare to puncture the myth of Australian goodness, daring to leap into the hypocrisy of race relations in Australia, from cruel schoolyard taunts, to the struggling Tongan boys, confined to the gumnut cottage and forced to appreciate their culture through creepy 'Polynesian Pathways'. This may be offensive to those who believe such programs promote civic happiness, but an important truth about regulation of ethnic culture in this country. Today's guerrilla satire is driven by the new technologies of digital cameras and internet distribution via Facebook, Twitter or YouTube, but the big difference is that the interactivity of these mediums allow a participation by consumers not seen in this country since the heydays of the *Bulletin*. Despite defamation laws, government threats to monitor the internet, a resurgent religious puritanism and the revival of patriotic correctness, the greatest danger to the larrikin spirit today is the dead hand of neoliberal corporatisation, paradoxically over-regulating our working, public and private lives beyond the dreams of the welfare state socialists of yesteryear. A somnolent bureaucracy built of metrics, key performance indicators and compliance that enlists a coercive homogenising notion of 'well-being' is smothering workplace dissent in so many of our great public and commercial institutions, even in those creative spaces such as universities and the media where troublemakers traditionally pushed back for the freedom to experiment, take risks and have fun.[24] But out in the 'burbs, online and in the back blogs, funny young people are busy self-curating extreme carnival to shock us awake from a conformist corporate version of happiness. Sometimes shocking, occasionally obscene, these larrikin agent provocateurs smuggle a sense of happiness – what former Prime Minister Paul Keating called 'Vaudeville' – into our otherwise utilitarian politics. But given the unequal distribution of happiness, we should not be surprised if the targets are not amused.

Endnotes

1   S. Ahmed, *The Promise of Happiness*, Duke University Press, Durham, 2010, p. 3.
2   ibid., p. 18.
3   J. Pilger, 'Days of Mourning in a Secret Australia', *The New Statesman*, 19 February 2007, viewed 13/5/2014, http://www.newstatesman.com/media/2007/02/pilger-australian-aboriginal.
4   T. Moore, *Dancing with Empty Pockets; Australia's Bohemians since 1860*, Pier 9, Millers Point, 2012, pp. 55–8, 190–3, 258–60.
5   M. Bakhtin, *Rabelais and his World*, trans. by Hélène Iswolsky, Indiana University Press, Bloomington, 1984, pp. 74, 78–9, 81.
6   J. Docker, *Postmodernism and Popular Culture: A Cultural History*, University of Cambridge, Melbourne, 1994, pp. 170–75.
7   See M. Belanta, *Larrikins: a History*, University of Queensland Press, St Lucia, 2012.
8   For a full account of Clarke's career see T. Moore, *Dancing with Empty Pockets: Australia's Bohemians since 1860*, Pier 9, Millers Point, 2012, pp. 7–42.
9   M. Clarke, *Peripatetic Philosopher*, Robertson, Melbourne, 1869, pp. 3–7, 11–13, 23–4, 29–30.
10 B. Elliot, *Marcus Clarke*, Oxford University Press, London, 1958, p. 202 and the *Age*, 7 December 1872, p. 4. See M. Clarke, 'Melbourne Cup', Melbourne *Herald*, 6 November 1873, in L. T. Hergenhan (ed.), *A Colonial City, High and Low Life: Selected journalism of Marcus Clarke*, University of Queensland Press, St Lucia, 1972, p. 184.
11 M. Clarke, 'The Future Australian Race', 1877, viewed 16/1/2015, http://www.telelib.com/authors/C/ClarkeMarcus/prose/AustalianTales/futureaustralian.html.
12 Clarke, *Peripatetic Philospher*, p. 34.

13 Moore, *Dancing*, pp. 55–8, 101–6.

14 S. Lawson, 'Print Circus', in A. Curthoys and J. Schultz (eds), *Journalism, Print, Politics and Popular Culture*, pp. 83, 90.

15 E. Ridell, interviewed by T. Moore, *Bohemian Rhapsody*, ABC TV, 1997.

16 D. Deamer, *The Queen of Bohemia: the Autobiography of Dulcie Deamer*, edited by P. Kirkpatrick, University of Queensland Press, St Lucia, 1998, p. 120.

17 ibid., p. 130.

18 See M. Heyward, *The Ern Malley Affair*, University of Queensland Press, St Lucia, 1994.

19 J. McAuley & H. Stewart, 'Ern Malley, Poet of Debunk', quoted in full in J. Tregenza, *Australian Little Magazines: 1923–1954: Their Role in Forming and Reflecting Literary Trends*, Libraries Board of South Australia, Adelaide, 1964, p. 66.

20 G. Greer, *The Female Eunuch*, Paladin, London, 1991, p. 25.

21 Moore, op. cit., pp. 261–2.

22 See T. Moore, *The Barry Mckenzie Movies*, Currency Press, Strawberry Hill, 2005.

23 B. Ellis, quoted in M. Harris, *Ockers: Essays on the Bad Old New Australia*, Maximus Books, Adelaide, 1974, p. 34.

24 Ahmed, op. cit., p. 3. Ahmed notes New Labour's happiness and 'social wellbeing' agenda in the United Kingdom.

THE RUSSIAN WAY OF HAPPINESS: ON LOVE, CHOICE AND COMMUNITY

Deborah Pike

In the final scene of Tchaikovsky's opera, *Eugene Onegin*, the eponymous hero sings to his beloved with all the fury of a man about to meet his end; that is, he is about to die of love. He begs the exquisite and darkly beautiful Tatyana – who, in her youth, offered him her heart without reserve – to finally flee with him. When she does not relent, he laments, stung with regret for having foolishly rebuffed her long ago. Tatyana is married to another man. And with all her tragic purity and virtue, she vows to remain faithful. It is simply too much. He is shanghaied into despair.

If Onegin had made a different choice long ago, and taken Tatyana as his wife, perhaps the dissolute hero would have been a happier man. Indeed, Tatyana's life appears so empty at the end, one imagines a more lively and passionate fate for her, had she escaped with her beloved. The plight of one of Russia's most cherished fictional heroes forces us to ponder the essence of Pushkin's tragedy – the loss entailed in making a decision that seals one's fate, and mourning the opportunity cost of that decision.

Celebrated Russian writers of the nineteenth century have much to say on the topic of happiness; with their moralist visions, they present us with a broad canvas of characters making decisions which impact dramatically upon their own destinies, as well as the lives of those around them. Reading these great novels is like tumbling into an immense web of event, choice, action and consequence, where the characters' pursuit of personal happiness above all else is radically thrown into question. The works of Pushkin, Tolstoy and Dostoyevsky reveal to us the paradox inherent in the search for happiness, they indicate that, not only is it undesirable, but it also makes us *unhappier.* Indeed, the most tragic figures are those deluded about what brings true happiness.

In his *Nichomachean Ethics,* Aristotle declared happiness to be the *summum bonum,* the ultimate good.[1] People may desire other things – such as fame, influence, love, wealth or beauty – because they believe that it will make them happy, however, their chief goal is to achieve this ultimate happiness. But if Aristotle is right, and we are driven to attain happiness above all else, then why do we so frequently make choices which do not lead to happiness? The problem appears to be with our definition of happiness, and therefore beliefs about what will make us happy. The more modern notion of happiness as a subjective state of well-being or satisfaction finds its roots in Sigmund Freud's idea of the pleasure principle, which can be described as our human instinct to seek pleasure and avoid pain in order to meet our biological and psychological needs.[2] This can be likened to hedonic happiness, which is pleasure-based. Aristotle's concept of *eudaimonia* or 'human flourishing' lies in contradistinction to these, offering a broader definition of happiness which includes moral, intellectual, as well as physical dimensions. Eudaimonia is a state of being which involves more than just personal contentment, rather, it necessitates the exercise of virtue and reason and maintaining quality social relations.[3] These Russian writers teach us that as long as we understand happiness as hedonic, rather than eudaimonic, our decisions will not make us happy.

The world of nineteenth-century aristocratic Russia may seem very different from our own: society was uncompromisingly stratified with virtually no possibility for social mobility and women had few liberties. One might imagine with the many limitations on freedom of choice, unhappiness would be everywhere. However, contemporary psychologists and philosophers of choice such as Dan Gilbert and Renata Salecl beg to disagree, arguing that today the situation is in fact far worse.[4] The sheer number of choices available to us in the Western developed world invoke the most incredible anxiety. Rather than bringing us happiness, they make us overwhelmed, paralysed and depressed. Today, the marketplace of twenty-first-century capitalism offers us seemingly limitless possibilities for choosing our identities and moulding our fates to please ourselves. Never before in history have we been provided with so many opportunities to fashion ourselves and our futures for the better. And yet, we are tyrannised by choice. Gilbert uses clinical examples demonstrating that when people are given fewer options, or are unable to reverse their decisions, they tend to accept what they have chosen, and are therefore happier with their lot.[5] He claims that decision-making has become so fraught that our significant choices – such as whether to get married and have children and so on – are influenced by the way we consider our future regrets.[6] Making a decision based on fear of regret is hardly a recipe for actively choosing happiness.

On the other hand, extrapolating from this to a world view that supports denying people choice is a recipe for oppression. In *The Second Sex*, Simone de Beauvoir writes that 'it is not too clear just what the word *happy* really means and still less what true values it may mask. There is no possibility of measuring the happiness of others and it is always easy to describe them as happy in the situation in which one places them.'[7] Generations of women and Russian serfs would doubtless agree.

Rational choice theory assumes that people choose what is in their best interests and maximise their own personal advantage. However, this is a fallacy, as human beings do not always act in their own interest even when they know what that is. We self-sabotage, deny ourselves what makes us happy so that the struggle can keep us alive: *I am conflicted therefore I am*. Psychoanalysis shows us that not everyone seeks obvious pleasures; some of us seek pain and often enough act against our well-being. Unconscious desires are in control particularly in the realm of romantic love and attraction; these cannot be rationally mastered. Some might argue that our choice of life-partner may well be based on an attempt to resolve the unmet needs of childhood. How can that possibly make us happy?

Life choices – such as where to live, what career to pursue, whom to marry or whether or not to have children – are often difficult, because what might make us happy now, may in fact not be what makes us happy later. Gilbert calls this phenomenon 'presentism', and argues that we make decisions for our future based on how we feel in the present.[8] Moreover, the problem with making decisions which have a bias towards our present inclinations, is that we fail to take into account how our needs and preferences change over time. A 17-year-old must decide on what career she will pursue, but after investing four years enrolled in interior architecture, discovers that she is bored. Decisions based on 'presentism' and feeling alone do not lead to joyous fates. Thinking more broadly about happiness, on the other hand, may.

As people are living longer and choices and options seem unbounded, how can we make sure we make the right choices? If it is impossible to predict how we will change in the future, how indeed, can we actually make decisions that will make us happy? Studies show that, as human beings, while we derive enormous pleasure from fantasising about our futures, and 'frolic[king] in the best of all imaginary tomorrows', we miscalculate, often imagining them to be rosier than they actually become.[9] There is something at fault then, in either our decision-making processes, or in our understanding of what truly satisfies us or makes us happy. Shakespeare is then correct, that '[t]he fault, dear Brutus, is not in our stars/ But in ourselves, that we are underlings.'[10] Literature provides us with ample opportunity to contemplate these dilemmas.

Alexander Pushkin's dry irony in *Onegin* lies partly in his central characters being a terrible match when they had the chance to marry, but having changed by the end of the story to become rather well suited, to no useful end, as they can no longer choose to be together. Pushkin's Onegin is a character whose decisions seem ad hoc. Positioning himself above convention, the intellectual, heir and dandy is both wayward and self-interested. He finds satisfaction in quoting the classics in order to bolster his wit and social prestige, he obsesses over his appearance, and teases women madly, and while 'he ha[s] keen perceptions', he 'on the whole despise[s] mankind'[11]. Not only does he dismiss the sincere affections of the worthy and intelligent Tatyana because he has no intention of 'marriage bonds or wedding bell'[12] but, in retaliation over the ensuing gossip of his refusal of her, flirts with her coquettish sister Olga. Outraged at his behaviour, her fiancé and his best friend, Vladmir Lensky, challenges him to a duel, where Onegin shoots his friend, unwillingly. This seemingly violent and random act culminates in his exile, and to some extent, his moral rehabilitation. He is so numbed with remorse he no longer cares for himself. Only upon seeing Tatyana many years on, does he realise his mistake. He is forced to live out his humiliation as his just reward for a life of seeking pleasure.

For Tatyana, Onegin first appears as an intriguing visitor to her country home, and rather like a character from one of the romantic stories she enjoys reading. She is so convinced of her love for him that she decides to take fate into her own hands and, astonishingly for a woman of her time, weaves her desire into a candid and poetic letter declaring her love. Upon meeting her weeks later, Onegin warns her against such openness, to 'Exercise restraint and reason/ For few will understand you so, /And innocence can lead to woe.'[13] But it is precisely Tatyana's innocence which shines throughout the tale and Onegin's guilt which hangs over it. In one of the novel's most poignant scenes, Tatyana visits Onegin's abandoned manor, and looks through his books wondering if Onegin did not model himself upon a series of fictional prototypes. She entertains the idea that perhaps he is not real at all: 'And in the margins she inspected/ His pencil marks with special care;/ And on those pages everywhere/ She found Onegin's soul reflected.'[14] Psychoanalyst Jacques Lacan teaches us that 'love itself…is addressed to a semblance'[15] and that our fantasy of what exists in the other is what makes love possible. Salecl seizes upon this, reminding us that, 'One of the timeless dilemmas…is that a person will often love in the other what the other does not actually possess – some sublime thing that the lover perceives in the beloved out of which he creates a fantasy that keeps his love alive.'[16] If fantasy is key to whom we choose to love and why we keep on loving, then a fantasised future – a 'semblance' is also at the heart of how we make our decisions.

Leo Tolstoy was a Russian nobleman who left high society to live on the land. His characters, too, make choices based on a fantasised perfection in the desired person, or on an imperfectly imagined future. *Anna Karenina* portrays some of Tolstoy's points of view on faith, work and love, as well as what constitutes true happiness. The novel begins with the famous maxim, 'All happy families are alike: each unhappy family is unhappy in its own way.'[17] Each family depicted in the novel experiences its own kind of unhappiness: the Oblonskys have money problems and infidelity to contend with; the Karenins are steeped in scandal; the Levins suffer from jealousy and discord.

The central drama in Tolstoy's epic is that of Anna Karenina, described as 'wife of one of the most important people in Petersburg…and a…*grande dame*'[18] and her affair with Count Vronsky, 'one of the finest examples of the gilded youth of Petersburg… Terribly rich, handsome, big connections…both cultivated and intelligent'.[19] He lavishes his attention on young Princess Kitty, but like Onegin, 'Marriage had never presented itself as a possibility.'[20] Levin, on the other hand, is described as 'awkward in society' and living a 'wild sort of country life busy with cattle'[21] and is in love with Kitty but she refuses to be his wife, believing Vronsky will propose. When Vronsky meets Anna, he notices her 'shining grey eyes' and 'thick lashes', her 'attentive' glance and 'restrained animation'. He is immediately taken with her: 'it was as if a surplus of something so overflowed her being that it expressed herself beyond her will, now in the brightness of her glance, now under her smile.'[22] This 'surplus' is passion, or feeling, and leads her to her peril.

Anna is dominated by her feelings: upon returning to her husband after meeting Vronsky, 'some unpleasant *feeling* gnawed at her heart. She was struck by the *feeling* of dissatisfaction with herself that she experienced on meeting him'[23] [my italics]. On the pure basis of her feeling, she leaves her husband for the debonair Vronsky, convinced that she can no longer keep up the 'state of pretences with her husband',[24] believing that her happiness lies with her lover. Little rational thought is involved in her decision – the dishonour to her husband, the impact on her son, risking her standing in society – all pale in comparison. Vronsky, too, is swept away with passion for Anna, 'He was so full of *feeling* for Anna that he did not even think what time it was'[25] [my italics]. Of the affair, Tolstoy writes that for 'Anna [it] had been an impossible, horrible, but all the more enchanting dream of happiness – this desire had been satisfied.' While she is sated, she 'felt herself so criminal and guilty'.[26] Her longing for a happiness based on personal satisfaction begins to sound so cheap. Anna is eventually shunned by her acquaintances.

While Anna Karenina is sympathetically portrayed by Tolstoy, she is nonetheless chastised for her selfishness through her suicide, or, as other readers may argue, the brutality of a cold society drives her to her death. Levin, on the other hand, eventually wins the heart of Kitty, and throws himself into a life of faithfulness, family and simplicity. One might decide that Tolstoy makes a statement that the moral life leads to happiness and the immoral life to unhappiness; indeed he approves of Levin's fidelity. Perhaps more subtly, however, the author presents the case that humans are social animals, and cannot flourish when isolated, and therefore choices that fail to take into account other people will result in sorrow. As such, he condones a happiness that is socially oriented and rationally based, one that is eudemonic, as opposed to hedonic. Love, however remains poignant in *Anna Karenina*: while it may be that Anna and Vronsky never become disillusioned with each other, or the love they share, Levin continues to experience melancholia, even as his life contains all he wants of it.

The idea of the happiness of the individual being thwarted by a mismatch between that person's character and the society he or she inhabits is common to many of the exalted Russian writers. Fyodor Dostoyevsky offers us a meditation on choice and happiness in his work, *The Idiot*, which centres on a personality unsuited to survive in this corrupt world. It is a chaotic novel, filled with many pages of arguing, intoxicated Russians, and the author pontificates about all manner of things, including the subject of writers, politics and – sure enough – the nature of choice and the pursuit of happiness.

While working on the novel, Dostoyevsky wrote a letter to his friend expressing his wish 'to depict a positively beautiful person'[27] in the character of Prince Lev Nikolayevich Myshkin. Prince Myshkin is one of the happiest protagonists in the history of the novel. The Prince is described as 'loyal without fawning', as having 'practical sense'[28] and 'a gaze...so gentle'[29]. He comes encumbered with nothing but 'a bundle of linen'[30] and he seems to immediately disarm many who meet him; indeed, he is liked even by those who hate him. The Prince is accused of being an 'innocent simpleton'[31] but he himself insists that he is 'intelligent all the same'.[32] While one character observes that he is a 'perfect child',[33] another remarks on the quality of his mind. One of the most striking features of his character is his lack of guile: unlike the conniving characters around him, the Prince is never manipulative or internally divided. Dostoyevsky is clear that he has created a 'holy fool', or a *yurodivy* as the Russians would say, a Christ-like figure in a society at war, in a vain and godless Russia.

The Prince wins the affections of two women in the novel: Agayla, the righteous and striking youngest daughter of the Epanchin family, to whom a multitude of men pay court, and with whom he spends much of his time, and the fallen yet bewitching Natasya Filippova, who tortures the men of the story, including the Prince's arch-rival Rogozhin, with her 'immeasurable beauty'[34] and capriciousness. Agayla is drawn to the Prince for many reasons, one is that he appears to possess the secret to happiness: 'Happy! You know how to be happy?'[35] she exclaims soon after meeting him, longing to be taught.

Natasya also falls in love with the Prince, but insists she cannot marry him because she wants him to be happy, and feels that he would never be so with her, but believes that Agayla would make him happy. She writes many crazed letters to Agayla, claiming the Prince's affections for her, and demanding that she must marry him. While the Prince is drawn to Agayla with a compassionate love, he only truly desires Natasya. After he accepts a proposal of marriage from Natasya, he denies that it will bring him contentment, pronouncing in shock, 'Happiness?

Oh no, not that.'[36] For the Prince, the pursuit of Natasya is a doomed one, after he chooses her over Agayla, he begins to lose his grip on reality.

The paradox of the Prince is that his seeming goodness draws others with him into a downward spiral. While Natasya meets her deadly end, so too Aglaya's life becomes tragic as she is later abandoned by a man claiming to be a Polish count. Dostoyevsky is suspicious of the pursuit of happiness; for him, people will always choose self-sabotage over what will truly make them happy. Pettiness and self-absorption lead to ruin. Social engagement, on the other hand, of the kind the Prince embarks upon, such as helping the poor and outcast, spending time with children, will be 'a cure for the soul.'[37]

At the beginning of the fourth volume of the work, Dostoyevsky avers that all people can be placed 'into two main categories: one limited, the other "much cleverer." The first are happier.'[38] Happiness is the gift of limited people, whereas those 'all infected from head to foot with the desire to be original' are 'much more unhappy than the first'.[39] While this could be taken as an ironic statement, it is perplexing, as the Prince shows that he is very intelligent yet at the same time naïve. In a sense, he manages to be both clever and happy and thus transcends the categories of person which Dostoyevsky delineates. The Prince's tragic end, however, shows that the two dispositions may well be impossible for any human being to maintain.

Indeed, happiness is not even unequivocally desirable in Dostoyevsky's world. In another of his works, *Notes from the Underground*, the narrator, a furtive philosopher–outcast, describes the pivotal importance of suffering and its relationship to human happiness:

Does not man, perhaps, love something besides well-being? Perhaps he is just as fond of suffering? Perhaps suffering is just as great a benefit to him as well-being? Man is sometimes extraordinarily, passionately, in love with suffering, and that is a fact, to care only for well-being seems to me positively ill-bred...suffering is the sole origin of consciousness...[it] is the greatest misfortune for man, yet I know man prizes it and would not give it up for any satisfaction.[40]

Happiness is not a moral ideal, but neither would it seem to be inherently immoral. And yet the pursuit of happiness can be enshrined by one culture (the USA) as a human right, and at the same time depicted by the artists of another culture as almost certain to be punished by misery and even death. In counter-poise to Aristotle's sense of happiness as the ultimate goal is the implication that happiness can only be gained as a by-product of a less self-centred activity, seen in work, loyalty, devotion to children, or more radically, acceptance of others as they are.

Poor Onegin is left alone at the end of Pushkin's novel-poem, but now instead of the self-chosen removal of the arrogant hedonist he suffers the imposed isolation of a man who missed his chance. Presentism caused him to reject Tatyana because he did not love her at that time, instead of imagining a future when he might come to love her. And yet here Tolstoy-approved consideration of the society they inhabited seems unlikely to lead to happiness for her, either. Perhaps they would both go on to embrace Dostoyevsky's passion for suffering. They, like most of the characters that appear in these stories, have sought happiness but instead gained wisdom.

Endnotes

1   Aristotle says, 'Assuming then that there is some one thing which alone is an end beyond which there are no further ends, we may call *that* the good of which we are in search.' see J. A. K. Thomson (ed), *The Ethics of Aristotle,* Harmondsworth, Penguin, 1966, p. 37.

2   S. Freud, *'Beyond the Pleasure Principle', 'Group Psychology' and Other Works, The Standard Edition of the Complete Psychological Works,* translated by J. Strachey & A. Freud, Vintage, London, 2001, vol. 18, p. 7. In *Civilisation and Its Discontents*, Freud writes, 'it is simply the programme of the pleasure principle that defines the purpose of life... What we call happiness in the strictest sense of the word comes from the fairly sudden satisfaction of pent-up needs.' S. Freud, *Civilisation and its Discontents*, Penguin, London, 2002, p. 16.

3   Aristotle takes pains to differentiate happiness from fleeting pleasure: 'any brief period of felicity does not make a man entirely and perfectly happy', *Ethics*, p. 39. He emphasises the importance of 'virtue, practical wisdom, speculative wisdom...[as] a source of pleasure in themselves', *Ethics*, p. 42, as well as friendship, as 'it is one of the things which in life we can afford to be without', *Ethics*, p. 227. Aristotle's *Ethics* is not without its problems, he insists that happiness 'must be perfect. This is why a man, if he is to be happy, must have in addition to his other advantages the physical advantages too, as well as external goods and the blessings of fortune – his activity must not be impeded through *lack* of these things, *Ethics*, p. 222. The idea that those who do not possess excellent health and fortune may not be happy is no doubt a limiting one.

4   See D. Gilbert, *Stumbling on Happiness*, Harper Perennial, London, 2007 and R. Salecl, *The Tyranny of Choice*, Profile Books, London, 2011.

5   Gilbert, *Stumbling on Happiness*, pp. 183–4.

6   ibid., p. 178.

7   S. de Beauvoir, *The Second Sex*, translated by H. M. Parshey, Picador, London, 1988, p. 28.

8   Gilbert, *Stumbling on Happiness*, p. 109.

9   ibid., p. 17.

10   W. Shakespeare, *The New Cambridge Shakespeare: Julius Caesar*, M. Spevack (ed.), Cambridge University Press, Cambridge, 2003, p. 85.

11   A. Pushkin, *Eugene Onegin: A Novel in Verse*, translated by James E. Falen, Oxford UP, Oxford, 1995, p. 41.

12   ibid., p. 41.

13 ibid., p. 89.

14 ibid., p. 167.

15 J. Lacan, *The Seminar of Jacques Lacan Book XX: On Feminine Sexuality: The Limits of Love and Knowledge 1972–1973*, J. Miller (ed.), translated by B. Fink, Norton, New York, 1998, p. 92.

16 Salecl, *The Tyranny of Choice*, p. 89.

17 L. Tolstoy, *Anna Karenina*, translated by R. Pevear & L. Volokhonsky, Penguin, London, 2003, p. 1.

18 ibid., p. 66.

19 ibid., p. 39.

20 ibid., p.57.

21 ibid., p. 43.

22 ibid., p. 61.

23 ibid., p. 104.

24 ibid.

25 ibid., p. 191.

26 ibid., p. 149.

27 F. Dostoyevsky, cited in J. P. Scanlan, *Dostoyevsky the Thinker*, Cornell UP, Ithaca, 2002, p. 152.

28 F. Dostoyevsky, *The Idiot*, translated by R. Pevear & L. Volokhonsky, Granta Books, London, 2003, p. 16.

29 ibid., p. 26.

30 ibid., p. 26.

31 ibid., p. 321.

32 ibid., p. 75.

33 ibid., p. 74.

34 ibid., p. 588.

35 ibid., p. 58.

36 ibid., p. 582.

37 ibid., p. 67.

38 ibid., p. 463.

39 ibid., p. 464.

40 F. Dostoyevsky, *Notes from Underground*, Planet Ebooks, p. 45.

AND THEY ALL LIVED HAPPILY EVER AFTER

Georgina Ledvinka and Anna Kamaralli

The cosiness of the child's experience of being tucked up at night, lulled to sleep by a bedtime story read by a kindly adult, largely rests on the dramas of the tale ultimately resolving into a happy ending. Whatever the story entails – be it castles and dragons, flights to outer space, or plucky girl detectives – and no matter what the perils, all will end well. The listener can thrill to the heroes' exciting adventures because, despite all the twists and turns, we know with quiet certainty that at the end of the tale they will live happily ever after. When children are set to do their own writing, intent with concentration as their chubby fingers grip thick pencils, we know that the story will probably begin with 'Once upon a time' and finish with the words 'And they all lived happily ever after. The End.' Adulthood brings with it the certain knowledge that life is messier than stories. From time to time we may experience shining outbursts of joy, or deep moments of quiet reflective satisfaction, but life continues after those peaks, and therefore does not deliver happy endings, if only because it does not deliver endings. Or at least, it only has one ending. As Margaret Atwood identified, 'The only authentic ending is the one provided here: *John and Mary die. John and Mary die. John and Mary die.*'[1] Narrative, on the other hand, requires a cutting-off point. The shape of the story arcs towards a moment that will be nominally designated the conclusion.

When a story is described as having a happy ending it is easiest to think of the happily-ever-after of a fairy tale. That is, the default story that produces the happy ending is romantic, heterosexual, and concluded at the point of marriage. But when did this become the default? The very idea of the happy ending as the appropriate literary fare for children is an illusion from practically every possible angle. Most fairy tales are full of darkness and violence, and as often as not do not end happily. Even more usually the characters do not all live happily ever after: the good do, while the bad are tortured with red-hot iron sandals. 'The good end happily, the bad unhappily, that is what fiction means,' as Oscar Wilde put it.[2] Almost all of his own fairy tales have miserable endings.

Until recently, stories for children have always had mottled conclusions. The heroines of Perrault and the Brothers Grimm are sometimes married off, and other times gobbled up; it is merely that their most famous tales have been the happy ones. *The Tales of the Arabian Nights* rely most often on adventures based around a bold young lad accumulating a fortune. Hans Christian Andersen's stories more often end in sorrow *(The Little Match Girl, The Steadfast Tin Soldier)* or are not about romance at all *(The Ugly Duckling, Little Claus and Big Claus)*. In the real world children have always experienced traumatic incidents, and have periodically inflicted them on their companions. The denial of this in choosing what stories to share with them says a great deal about what adults want to believe about childhood, rather than speaking to children's own understanding of the world.

We conceive of childhood, at least in the contemporary Western world, as a period of innocence and happiness that must be protected at all costs. Many of our social and legal systems are built around it, and myriad laws and organisations exist for the purpose of protecting children from physical and mental ills that may occur at the hands of those around them. When the system falls down, and we hear of a child who has been abused or otherwise mistreated, we are horrified not only by the terrible experience they have gone through but also by the idea that they have been robbed of the innocence and happiness that is their right as a child, and thus there has been a compounding of the level of damage inflicted. Unfortunately, this has at times allowed harm to come to children because adults have been unable to face the idea that someone has chosen to harm them.

Examining the history of attitudes to child labour does much to illuminate broader shifts in how childhood is perceived. The idea of child labour is now assumed to be abhorrent, and recent years have seen an increase in ethical shopping movements such as World Vision Australia's 'Don't Trade Lives' campaign that seeks to reduce the market in Australia for products manufactured through child labour.[3] And yet we allow it to continue as long as we do not have to see it around us.

During the British Industrial Revolution, in the late eighteenth and early nineteenth centuries, a combination of factors (including advances in technology, high dependency ratios within families, faltering male wages and poverty) meant that employment of children in Britain was commonplace, rife, even, in areas most severely affected by poverty.[4] Historian Jane Humphries notes that children were regularly employed not only in mills and mines but also in agriculture, factories and domestic work, often for very poor wages, and thus, she says, 'child labour was a major contributing factor in Britain's industrialization.'[5] A child could be employed from the age of seven, a hangover from that age being, in earlier eras, the time a boy child was 'breeched', that is, put in pants instead of petticoats, removed from the nursery, and sent into apprenticeship or to be squire to a knight. In textile factories the littlest ones would be given the job of crawling under the weaving machines to retrieve the fallen scraps of wool. This was the most dangerous job in the factory, as the chance of having fingers or hair caught in the machines was high. There was no sense that the greater vulnerability of the youngest should result in greater measures to protect them.

With the rise of Romanticism – an intellectual, literary and artistic movement that began at the end of the eighteenth century and spread throughout Western Europe, reaching its peak in the 1850s – new ways of thinking about children emerged. The Romantics began to envisage childhood as a particular passage in life, distinct from adulthood, with its own qualities and experiences.[6] Romantic intellectuals pondered questions about what made children different from adults, and what particular needs they might have in order to mature successfully. Among the ideas they developed were notions that children are closer than adults to nature and to God, and that children possess inherent innocence as they have not yet been assimilated into the workings of society in the same manner as adults. Jean-Jacques Rousseau idealised the infant because it had yet to be shackled by civilisation. These ideas are reflected in Romantic literature such as William Blake's *Songs of Innocence and of Experience*

(1789–1794). Blake challenged the acceptability of child labour in two poems which lay bare the miseries suffered by chimney sweeps. In *Songs of Innocence*, Blake writes from the perspective of a young boy who has been sold into the trade:

> When my mother died I was very young,
> And my father sold me while yet my tongue
> Could scarcely cry "Weep! weep! weep! weep!"
> So your chimneys I sweep, and in soot I sleep.[7]

In the poem, a boy named Tom envisages 'thousands of sweepers...all of them locked up in coffins of black,' but then he dreams that:

> ...by came an angel, who had a bright key,
> And he opened the coffins, and set them all free;
> Then down the green plain, leaping, laughing, they run
> And wash in a river, and shine in the sun.[8]

However, even here Blake concludes that the little sweeps will be happy if each does his best at his work, which shows he was not prepared to go so far as to advocate openly for the abolishment of this form of child servitude. The poem ends with the chimney sweeps rising to begin a working day, and the line 'So if all do their duty they need not fear harm', which is hardly a searing condemnation of what they are being forced to do. Blake's poem provides a clear statement of the Romantic concept, derived from Rousseau, of childhood being intimately connected with godliness and nature, and with the idea of carefree, happy innocence being something children deserve.

However, he falls short of actually calling for the real world to offer that to all children, perhaps hoping the reader's conscience will be pricked without such an explicitly activist statement. It is an illusion that the Romantics' idealisation of childhood innocence ended child servitude; in fact it extended well into the later nineteenth century and beyond. George Bernard Shaw was still writing plays criticising the way the British put their children into slave labour in the 1890s,[9] and in Australia, the employment of children peaked as late as 1940 with 34,000 children making up 6 per cent of the total number of factory workers at the time.[10] By the early twentieth century, the sending of children out to work had not ceased, but had become heavily stratified by class, which is more or less how the practice continues today, on a world scale.

As literary scholar Ann Rowland observes, the ideas associated with childhood that emerged in the Romantic period have become foundational to the dominant cultural and historical paradigms of the nineteenth and twentieth centuries, and thus, for a significant period of time, they have strongly influenced our understanding of the world.[11]

Because Romantic and romanticised notions of childhood are still so pervasively accepted in the West, we resist assimilating the idea of a child who does not comply with this norm, even when we should know better. Nobel Prize–winning author William Golding gained notoriety at least in part because he chose children as his characters for his 1954 novel *Lord of the Flies*, which tells the story of a group of pre-adolescent boys who find themselves marooned in wartime on a tropical island, when a plane that was evacuating them crashes. Very quickly the apparent idyll of the island descends into horror as most of the boys succumb to mob rule and carry out bloodthirsty acts of brutality against the others. This sees its culmination in the murder of Piggy, an overweight, bespectacled boy, always the easiest type to 'other' and exclude, whose brains they dash out with a rock. Golding's message about human savagery bubbling beneath a thin surface layer of civilisation is undoubtedly heightened by his use of children as the protagonists. The novel's ghastly portrait of childhood barbarity mocks Rousseau's picture of nature as virtuous, while making closer-to-home demands that the reader confront the illusion of believing children to be inherently without malice. Everybody has been through childhood and therefore, if we are honest, we all know the limits to its innocence. The vicious cruelty displayed by the gang of boys is a reminder that few people experienced their peers as uniformly gentle and accepting. Many readers will have experienced bullying or mean behaviour from children, or did less than innocent things themselves in their own 'innocent' years.

The question for parents and teachers of children lucky enough to live comfortable lives turns on the tension between the desire to give children a period of their lives unburdened by worries, and the need to help them develop empathy. How much are we prepared to let the ones who avoid suffering know that it exists? Or that some never escape it? Certainly stories for very young children hold to the principle of the happy ending almost without deviance. Primary-school-age children will only rarely be shown sorrow without eventual rescue, but the exceptions are noteworthy. Some children's literature is specifically directed at helping children tackle the kinds of problems they are likely to face, with specialist stories on things such as bullying, illness or acquiring a new sibling. *Old Pig*, for example, is aimed squarely at primary-school-age children, introducing the idea of coping with the death of a loved one.[12] A happy ending for these books means resolving the specific issue at hand, or finding acceptance of an unavoidable situation.

Eleanor Coerr's *Sadako and the Thousand Paper Cranes*, in which the young heroine never gets her wish to be cured of leukaemia, provides about the earliest introduction to a genuinely sad ending in a children's novel.[13] Not only the death of the child protagonist, but the failure of fate to reward her for her dedication to her ritual task, folding a thousand origami cranes, runs counter to the principles of fairy tale. A slightly different case is the devastating *The Boy in the Striped Pyjamas*. This is not strictly speaking a book written for children, but as told in the first person by a child, the language and conceptual level of the protagonist makes it accessible to nine and ten year olds. Like the story of Sadako, the book can be used to introduce children to some of the horrific events arising from World War II, but the conclusion in which the narrator chooses to die with his friend in a gas chamber pushes too far for most. Tom Donegan of the Oxford Story Museum reports that it is common to hear of primary school teachers reading this book aloud to their classes, but simply omitting the final chapter.[14]

A few children's books deliberately subvert the expectation of happy endings, playing on everybody's knowledge of their dominance. Lemony Snicket repeatedly disavows any prospect of happy endings and implores those looking for them to go elsewhere. 'I'm sorry to say that the book you are holding in your hands is extremely unpleasant.'[15] Snicket's series teeters on the cusp of novels that are still for children, before books tip into the grittier world of Young Adult literature. Here narrative outcomes become increasingly complex, and these novels tend to be quite brave about realistic, or even dystopian endings.

The awarding of one of the most prestigious children's literary awards, the Carnegie Medal, to Kevin Brooks' *The Bunker Diary*, a book with no happy ending, in which the protagonist dies without ever resolving a meaning for his suffering at the hands of a psychopath, prompted some serious reflection on what children should be exposed to.[16] Brooks said in his acceptance speech that 'As readers, children – and teens in particular – don't need to be cosseted with artificial hope that there will always be a happy ending.' However, the intense discussion surrounding the book often slid over the key point made by one of its chief critics. Amanda Craig, writing in British newspaper the *Independent*, suggested that books for adolescents should not show a world devoid of hope or the possibility of meaningful action.[17] Brooks responded as if he were being asked to write stories with no conflict: '*The Bunker Diary* is a book about dark and disturbing subjects – it has to contain dark and disturbing things.'[18] There is a distinction to be made between a denial of suffering and a denial of hope.

So if fairy tales are prepared to end unhappily, and so are books designed as literature for children, where did we get the impression that a happy ending is the norm? Fairy tales are dark, violent and often morally questionable. Not only do they only sporadically end happily, but even the ostensibly happy ones often involve brutality and death for the villain, and very likely a few others along the way. To find where we are getting the impression that fairy tales end happily we must come back up from examining their medieval roots, and see where they have blossomed in recent decades. It is not actually classic children's stories that insist on happy endings, but rather their modern movie versions. It is Hollywood that cannot abide the idea of anything less than perfect happiness, for fairy tales always have happy endings in their movie incarnations. Tales told to children have always had a purpose. Broadly speaking they have always been selling something. The recent shift is that instead of selling caution or respect for elders, they are selling actual merchandise, and while a sad outcome may sell obedience, it will not sell action figures. It is significant that the original ending of Hans Christian Andersen's *The Little Mermaid* was sad, and changed by Disney for the film. In the original version the Prince never falls in love with the mermaid, but marries someone else. The Disney version is now so famous, and so many people have grown up with it, that it seems to have been almost forgotten that the heroine ever failed to win her man.

Children's stories are not in fact the chief means by which Western society circulates the comforting idea that life is all about happy endings – that no matter what happens, we can look forward to the prospect of living happily ever after. By far the biggest and most influential purveyor of this notion is the Hollywood movie industry, and it sells this message to adults. Parents take their children to the movies, and they want to experience the day out as an escape. Movies take considerable money to make, and a happy ending is by far the safest investment.

Arguably the success of Hollywood action films lies in their ability to deliver audiences (in exchange for a relatively modest financial outlay) utter escapism, the razzamatazz of special effects, and feats of superhuman daring and endurance, with all of the plot's thrills and spills safely wrapped up in a narrative package that guarantees a 'happily ever after' ending. No matter what

Chris Pine, Harrison Ford, Tom Cruise – insert name of white American male A-list actor *du jour* – is required to do, the audience knows he will manage it; he will defeat the enemy, save the world, get the girl(s), and all the while he will be enviably suave. James Bond may be in his early sixties (following the publication of the first 007 novel, *Casino Royale*, in 1953)[19] but he still has the body and never-give-up attitude of chiselled, forty-something hard man, Daniel Craig. Similar rules apply in Hollywood romantic comedies. Cinemagoers know that whatever goofy mishaps may befall the pleasant-looking lead male and his subtly sexy, girl-next-door counterpart, along with their oddball supporting cast of likeable misfits, love will triumph over adversity: boy and girl will admit the inevitability of their attraction, resolve their differences, and live together in blissful joy forever more.

No wonder these movies are appealing, and that occasionally even the most dedicated arthouse film buff will succumb to their lure, despite knowing that Hollywood blockbusters invariably reinforce the status quo by perpetuating Western hegemonies that privilege notions such as capitalism, whiteness, masculinity and heterosexuality above all else. It begins to seem more likely that the insistence of mainstream movies on a happy ending has seeped into what we offer to children, rather than that children's stories have influenced the movies. But as long as children have access to books as well as mainstream films, there is scope for them to experience that neatly resolved, happily-ever-after endings are only one aspect of storytelling, and that many other, more complicated outcomes are possible. It would not hurt us to admit, also, that what children give us is the opportunity to pretend belief in happy endings. Perhaps there is nothing so terribly wrong with using our children to indulge in dreams of happiness while we may. By telling ourselves that things will end well, we can be like the child who drifts happily off to sleep, cocooned by a warm sense that all is right with the world.

Endnotes

1   M. Atwood, 'Happy Endings', in *Murder in the Dark*, Coach House Books, 1983.

2   O. Wilde, *The Importance of Being Ernest*.

3   World Vision, 'Don't Trade Lives', undated, viewed 9 May 2014, http://campaign.worldvision.com.au/campaigns/dont-trade-lives/.

4   J. Humphries, 'Childhood and child labour in the British Industrial revolution', *Economic History Review*, vol. 66, no. 2, 2013, pp. 395–418, at p. 395.

5   Humphries, *Economic History Review*, p. 400.

6   A. W. Rowland, *Romanticism and Childhood: The Infantilization of British Literary Culture*, Cambridge University Press, Cambridge, 2012, p. 7.

7   W. Blake, 'The Chimney-Sweeper', in W. B. Yeats (ed.), *William Blake, Collected Poems*, Routledge, London and New York, 2002, p. 51.

8   Blake, *Collected Poems*, p. 51.

9   G. B. Shaw, *The Man of Destiny*, 1896.

10 Australian Bureau of Statistics, 'A Century of Change in the Australian Labour Market', *Year Book Australia, 2001*, http://www.abs.gov.au/AUSSTATS/abs@.nsf/Previousproducts/1301.0Feature%20Article142001.

11 Rowland, *Romanticism and Childhood*, p. 10.

12 M. Wild and R. Brooks, *Old Pig*, Puffin, London, 1999.

13 Eleanor Coerr, *Sadako and the Thousand Paper Cranes*, Puffin, London, 1977.

14 In interview with Anna Kamaralli, 8 September 2014, by phone.

15 D. Handler, *Lemony Snicket's A Series of Unfortunate Events*, Harper Collins, New York, 1998.

16 Quoted in A. Flood, *Guardian*, 24 June 2014, http://www.theguardian.com/books/2014/jun/24/carnegie-medal-the-bunker-diary-kevin-brooks.

17 A. Craig, *Independent*, 25 June 2014, http://www.independent.co.uk/arts-entertainment/books/features/the-bunker-diary-should-books-have-happy-endings-9560752.html.

18 A. Flood, *Guardian*, 24 June 2014, http://www.theguardian.com/books/2014/jun/24/carnegie-medal-the-bunker-diary-kevin-brooks.

19 I. Fleming, *Casino Royale*, Jonathan Cape, London, 1953.

3

PERSONAL ENCOUNTERS

AFTER ZERO

Alice Pung

'Doctor, I ate one of those creatures', my grandmother blurted out one day at our doctor's office in suburban Melbourne, pointing to a chiropractic poster on the wall, 'We ate them when we were starving'. Granny was in her eighties at this time, a survivor of revolution in China and then the Killing Fields of Cambodia. Her mind was still as sharp as a digital photograph, but her eyesight was not as clear as it once was. My father, aunty and I looked at the chart, alarmed and embarrassed.

'Mother, that's a spine!' laughed my aunty.

'Huh? But we ate creatures that looked exactly like that', my grandmother protested.

'That's a picture of a human spine on its side', explained my father, 'What you're thinking of are centipedes'.

'Yes. That's right, centipedes', mused my aunty, 'Come to think of it, they do look a lot like that picture up there on your wall, doctor'.

I waited for what usually happened when granny made such admissions. I waited for her to list to our good doctor all the things they ate while they were starving: crickets, scorpions, rodents, even my father's leather belt, which they cut into small pieces and boiled for hours on end in secret, to tenderize it. I waited for them to laugh about all this – this secret joke of shared experience – while the doctor and I watched in wonder.

I had always known that my father survived the Killing Fields of Cambodia. I'd grown up with adults around me talking incessantly of the Black Bandits, which is what they called their captors, the Khmer Rouge soldiers who dressed in black, because colour was banned. I knew how this story ended, because it always ended on a good note. What 5-year-old could fail to be enamoured of a story that culminated in her own birth? Manufactured in a Thai refugee camp, but assembled in Australia with Chinese parts, I was named Alice after Alice in Wonderland, because my father thought this country was one.

My parents taught me not to cry when I had to get immunisations, not through fear or the promise of lollies, but through their own stoicism. They talked about human backbone and starvation diets as if they were everyday memories – for them, these things were just as ordinary as remembering the 1977 Rugby World Cup, finding out about Elvis's death or listening to ABBA songs were for everyday Australians during that time. They never spoke about their experiences to shock strangers or endear themselves to sympathetic ears. They never spoke about them to anyone outside our family unless asked, or if my grandmother blurted revelations out at doctors' offices. 'Remember Needle?' my mother might say to my father over dinner one evening, 'Remember how talented she was with a sewing machine? She could just look at an outfit and then go to the New Market, find the cloth, and copy it exactly'.

'Too bad she was smashed', my father would say, and they would both sigh and continue eating dinner.

Yet my father did not seem to be burdened by his past. He didn't understand what posttraumatic stress disorder was, or survivor's guilt. Those were feelings for people who had time to feel feelings instead of getting down to work and making the most of this miraculous new life, this life after seeing death so close. So he named me Alice, and then the rest of my siblings followed suit with the first letter of the alphabet: Alexander, Alison, Alina. When cousins started to arrive from overseas or were born here, they too were given 'A' names: Angelina, Angel, Anderson, Amanda, Amara. It didn't matter what part of Asia or Southeast Asia they had come from, they too were going to fulfil this narrative of new beginnings.

My father bought me watercolours and charcoals from a real artists' supply store, not children's crayolas and textas. He wanted me to make art in my life, not just scribbles. He also made us toys. He knew how to make Clag, play dough, and apples out of balloons. He taught me how to do calligraphy. For too long, his life had been bereft of culture and art. But my favourite toy was the egg roly poly. He would hollow out a raw egg, fill it halfway with wax, and draw a face on it with a pen. Every time you knocked the roly poly over, it would sway from side to side before standing back upright. You could never knock it down unless you smashed it. It reminded me of my father's resilience.

So when I began writing my book about my father six years ago, I understood the gravitas of the task of interviewing him about his experiences in Cambodia. He had survived one of the most far-reaching experiments in social engineering of the last century, Pol Pot's Year Zero, a regime as literal as it sounds. Pol Pot named himself after the phrase 'Political Potential' and he decided that in order to implement a pure Marxist regime and efface all traces of the traitorous modern world, he had to drag time back to Year Zero. The French had attempted a similar thing, calling the first day of their new postrevolutionary regime in 1789 Year One; Pol Pot took it one step further.

His regime banned laughter and smiling. It banned crying too. Everyone wore black. Music was also banned. Hospitals did not exist. Modern medicine did not exist. Technology did not exist – no running water, no electricity, not even soap or toothbrushes. The only permissible personal property was an individual spoon. People were shot simply for knowing a foreign language or wearing glasses. All the things that we think make for a happy life – interest in the larger world, medical and scientific advances, free expression of our feelings – were executable offences. 'To spare you is no profit, to destroy you is no loss' was the motto of the regime.

I had talked to psychologists and academics about genocide survivors, consulted with older Jewish friends, studied up on the ethics and sensitivities of approaching victims, read every study of the Cambodian genocide that I could find. If I was going to write a book about a survivor, I wanted to do it the right way.

But most of my father's stories I already knew from dinner discussions and having grown up with aunties, uncles and friends who were also survivors. 'There was a truck that drove by, with bodies for burial stacked on top of each other behind the wire grating', my father's colleague would say at lunchtime at the Retravision store where we all worked, 'And as the truck passed me, I could see that *some of the limbs were still moving*'. And then another person would tell us that in their camp the soldiers would cut open people's stomachs while they were still alive, to see if they had been stealing rice. And half an hour later, back to work we would go. We'd stand on the shop floor smiling, selling whitegoods and browngoods and mobile phones to customers, happily explaining the marvels of modern technology to those who mostly took these things for granted.

The stories of great horror my father told me did not entirely surprise me. By then I'd also read almost every single memoir about surviving the Killing Fields that had been translated into English, from Haing S Ngor's autobiography to Bizot's *The Gate*, as well as the works of David Chandler and Ben Kiernan. Yet the one moment that took me most by surprise was when my father suddenly told me, 'There were some happy moments too'.

'What do you mean happy moments?' I asked.

'Well, you know, when I got promoted to the fertilizer team'.

One evening my father had been dragged out of his hut by two soldiers with guns. He realised it was probably going to be his end, in the dark of the night, without being able to say goodbye to his mother or sister. He was taken to the unit commander's hut. 'You can do acupuncture, is that true?' the soldiers yelled at him. My father didn't know whether he should confess or stay quiet – either way, he would be smashed. He had found some electrical wires, stripped the plastic covering from them and sharpened the copper tips to a fine point. This was how he secretly practised acupuncture and treated the sick.

'Yes', he confessed to the soldiers, 'I do acupuncture'.

They pointed to the unit commander who was writhing about in bed with terrible stomach pains. 'Get your needles out', they commanded him.

The next day, the commander was sitting up in bed eating rice porridge, and he gave my father a promotion. Instead of working in the fields, my father got the easiest job in the collective, which was to collect and make fertiliser with human excrement. 'We sang songs', my father reminisced, 'I was surrounded by all these beautiful women'. Only the women the soldiers found most endearing were sent to this unit so that they would not have to toil in the sun. 'We sang when no soldiers were around'.

My father returned to Cambodia and saw one of his 'sisters' from the fertiliser team again. By then she was a grandmother in an enormous, double-storey gated house with a polished wooden ceiling. They had not seen each other in thirty years. She was rotund and regal. My father told me, 'This lady used to be a real beauty when she was young. She had the voice of a songbird, too'. It sounded like something you would say about your friend who had a former career as a model or small screen actress, not your fellow slave worker who mixed human excrement with you day in and day out while you all starved.

My father also told me about the day his collective of thousands of people received a tin of Nestle sweetened condensed milk. In the medieval hell that was Pol Pot's Cambodia, that tin of sweetened condensed milk was a solitary ambassador of the modern world. One 395 mL tin mixed into an enormous 100 L black pot, with all those vassal-faced, black clothed, starving men and women looking on, slackened jaws and hungry eyes, as the pot was stirred, holding out their bowls and spoons in anticipation and excitement.

Then there was the day when my father thought he saw the work of the Buddha. One day while toiling in the fields, he watched a bird peck at a pond of water – more a puddle, really – and emerge with what looked like a fish in its mouth. As the bird flew off, the fish fell back onto the earth, and my father collected it. That day was also granny's birthday.

In my ignorance, I had not realised that a human being who has been starved and enslaved for four years might not have lasted that long but for hope. Happiness seemed to be an act of defiance against hopelessness.

My father's motto was 'Never look back on what was lost, always face forwards'. He got angry when one of his homesick friends told him, 'Our bodies are in Australia, but our heads and hearts are turned towards China'. No, he insisted, you can't think this way. Such ingratitude! Happiness was to always be thankful for small and large miracles.

There is a character in Ha Jin's novel *A Free Life*, in which the wife of the writer-protagonist says that her idea of happiness would be for one day to pass into the next, and be the same as the last. And for a while, for my parents, happiness was the same as comfort. They marvelled over running hot tap-water, indoor plumbing, occupational health and safety laws, traffic lights, escalators, McDonalds stores, Nescafé. They stocked up on tins of their precious Nestle sweetened condensed milk. They marvelled over the clothes they received from the Brotherhood of St Lawrence, they 'wahh'ed over monuments such as the Shrine of Remembrance and the Arts Centre. They fell in love with each other again and with this new country. One of my friends once told me, 'That kind of love doesn't sound like falling in love. That sounds like falling in relief'.

It is true.

My parents fell blissfully into relief.

When I was twenty-five, I went on my first silent Buddhist retreat. We surrendered our phones at the door, were not allowed to talk to one another for the whole five days, and had to be very mindful of our every action. We woke up at five in the morning – and sometimes, four-thirty – did yoga exercises, cleaned out the retreat centre, sat meditating for hours crossed-legged or in full lotus position, cooked our own meals, cleaned the windows and floors. If we fell asleep during our meditation, a monk would hit us on the back with a large stick. So we had to concentrate. At times I had to stand up to meditate because I was so tired.

'Are you mad?' laughed my father when I came back, 'You voluntarily gave up freedom of speech and movement and spent five days under the threat of the whacking stick? Sounds a bit like the Khmer Rouge to me'.

The Buddha, like many of the victims of the Khmer Rouge, was a wealthy, sheltered man who lost his wealth. Unlike the victims, he voluntarily let go of it, it was not stolen from him. The Buddha tried to gain enlightenment by starving himself until he could feel his backbone through his stomach. He then discovered the middle path, of not living in extremes; and he came up with the four noble truths:
1. There is suffering
2. There is a cause to suffering
3. There is an end to suffering
4. There is a path to the end of suffering

Buddha himself said, 'We are what we think. All that we are arises with our thoughts. With our thoughts we make the world'. Each noble truth has at its heart the concept of *dukkha*, which means 'suffering' or 'unsatisfactoriness' in Pali. Put another way, Buddhists believe that suffering is inevitable. Anything that is not permanent, that is subject to change, is *dukkha*. Thus, happiness contains within it the seeds of *dukkha*. Great success, which fades with the passing of time, is also *dukkha*.

Western Buddhists don't like this focus on *dukkha*, just as Western psychology does not like to focus on negativity. In this new, developed, comfortable and secure world in which my parents brought me up, it appears that we are trying to eliminate all traces of suffering. Some have even gone to the opposite extreme in conceptualising Buddhism, to position the Noble Truths more positively: There is Happiness. There is a cause of Happiness. There is a way of Happiness. There is a path to Happiness. Yet this focus on attaining happiness seems a more elusive and nebulous quest. After all, everyone knows what suffering is. It is universal and something we can all identify in ourselves and others. Yet how do we identify or qualify happiness?

The Khmer Rouge banned religion and killed monks. They took the Buddha's four noble truths and reduced them to two, and of those first two noble truths, they stretched them to their perverse literal extremes, so that they would snap back and slap you in the face. All life is suffering. *You* are the cause of the suffering. You must be punished with more suffering. The Khmer Rouge regime banned unauthorised feeling.

Now that we can feel all we want, we are no longer content with small joys – the comfort that every day may unwind like the last – but we must have our large excitements. The idea that happiness is tantamount to excitement is the crux of all consumerist advertisements: Riveting new do-it-yourself home hair-dye colours. A car that will change your life. Swimming with sharks at the aquarium. Even cruise ships for wealthy geriatric retirees are premised on the idea of seeing the Amalfi Coast as never before, or finding something novel in an oft-visited place. Do new memories need to be made constantly, like a factory production quota, in order for us to be 'surprised by joy'?

My father's Retravision business grew larger and larger, especially in the economic boom of the '90s. Suddenly, my mother found herself smack bang in the middle of the suburbs in a massive house. What a house. They had spent one and a half decades working for this. No longer was waste left in a cesspit for my father to collect, now we could think which one of our four toilets to use. No longer did they live in the dark, sleep hundreds-and-thousands-to-a-thatched-roof; but with the flick of a switch could have a light on at all times of the night until daybreak. No longer did they have to grow or forage for every piece of food that entered their mouths, we had modern miracles such as microwaves and fruit extractors. We even had a machine that cut cling wrap for us on a heated strand of metal wire. The meaning of human existence was no longer condensed and confined to the length of a starving man's digestive tract, but expanded to his comfort, his ease, his rest. Upstairs we had a leather chair that, when you flicked a switch, would shiatsu-massage your limbs and lumbar spine; downstairs we had a fridge that made ice on demand.

Yet the more affluent my parents became, the more paranoias they entertained. When I was in primary school, they used to let me catch the bus by myself to do grocery shopping in the next suburb. Now, my younger sisters were driven everywhere. We lived in what was probably the safest cul-de-sac in the state, but that did not assuage their fears. They had never had it so safe, and yet they felt constant external threats to their safety. My father took to reading Andrew Bolt, my mother took to wandering the shopping centre to line our lives with new bath soaps and fleecy towels. My parents' fears were not only post-traumatic war-related ones, I realised. It was also that now the more they had, the more they felt they had to lose.

Fear, according to Buddhists, is the root of the other negative states of mind, like envy, and arrogance and hatred. Reduce your fear, and you reduce the amount you covet your neighbour's things, your pride and your strong feelings towards your enemies. You also reduce your need to cling onto things, or hoard, or read fear-cultivating newspaper columnists. 'It is not power that corrupts but fear', wrote Aung San Suu Kyi in *Freedom From Fear*, 'Fear of losing power corrupts those who wield it and fear of the scourge of power corrupts those who are subject to it'.

There is a German word, *weltschmerz*, which means 'sorrow that one feels and accepts as one's necessary portion in life'. In that Buddhist retreat, I learned that life is only as long or as short as your next breath. The four noble truths are called 'noble', not unpleasant, or intolerable or awful. Eliminate all traces of suffering and you eliminate what it means to be human.

I remember inviting my father to speak to some of my students at college ten years ago, when I was a political science tutor. He demonstrated on a student how a 10-year-old girl's hands were tied behind her back by the Khmer Rouge, and how they flopped uselessly when the binds were finally released. He talked about performing the acupuncture that restored her hands again, matter-of-factly, not meaning to take any life-saving credit.

One of my students asked him: 'Why weren't you depressed?'

My father shrugged. This was as honest as he could come to answering his own question of suffering: 'You just get through it. Your family might still be alive'.

'It is incredible', my student later told me, 'how a man like that is walking around in ordinary life'.

Suddenly, I saw exactly what he meant. I realised I had been living with someone who survived, an *extraordinary* person in every day of my everyday life. Yet I knew that the real miracle wasn't the survival. The real miracle was that he could still see the *extra* in the *ordinary*, and find happiness in small things. The real miracle was that he could still love.

ON THE CANCER WARD

Ranjana Srivastava

After only our fourth meeting she relays to me that she is reconciled to death but will fight until the last to preserve quality of life. This is why she declined chemotherapy for cancer diagnosed at an advanced stage – she chose to spend her remaining days with her daughter and husband.

They have taken her to every local beach and some far-away ones and every playground they can think of, each photo of the event annotated with a special message. 'The volunteers offered to help create memorabilia but I want my daughter to know that I did this all by myself. Although, it will never replace all the sandwiches I won't make and the assemblies I won't attend'. She says, 'I know that I won't be here to see her start school in a few months. I have spoken to her teachers and I just have to trust that everyone else, the whole school, will be the mother she won't have. And of course, she has a wonderful dad. She will be in good hands with him'.

At this, I choke, surreptitiously pinching the skin of my hand to remain steadfast. I remind myself that an observer like me is not entitled to subsume her grief: it is not etiquette and moreover, it feels self-indulgent.

But of course, I too have a little girl like my patient's who is turning five. She too starts school next year and we have been attending orientation, her eyes filled with wonder that suddenly she will possess dozens of new friends, a brand new school uniform and the same blue hat that her big brother won't let her borrow. Just yesterday we picked out a pink lunch box and a matching pink water bottle and made a list of foods she can take to school. 'I guess you can't fill the fruit section with chocolate buttons', she observed before declaring, 'My teacher will know, she just will'.

I managed to make it to every single orientation class, never even entertaining the possibility that anyone else in our family, including her father or grandparents might be interested in going. In the way of the all-consuming love a mother feels for her child, I did it all and did it willingly. And what fun we had there, I think, even as I ward off the thoughts – lest they magically appear on my forehead for my patient to read.

But the truth is that I didn't have to stop at the side of the playground to clutch my hurting side and I didn't have to fish for the omnipresent bottle of morphine to rescue me before I could move again. And when the children played catch, I joined in, rather than sitting on the bench while my little girl explained to strangers that her mummy needed all the oxygen she could get to keep her breathing. My interview with my daughter's teacher was about purely benign, happy things. I did not need to entrust her with the heartbreaking responsibility of being my child's surrogate mother.

'I am sorry', I say, contritely. 'I am sorry that you are so ill. It's not fair'.

'What can you do? It was meant to be', she replies.

'How are *you* doing?' I ask her husband. He has given up work to care for her.

'I feel sad for the life that we won't have. I had always thought we'd grow old together'. His eyes shine with tears. She holds his hand.

'I am not afraid of dying', she says. 'I have a strong faith and I trust God is waiting for me. So while it's a bit premature, heaven is a good destination'. I find her poise enormously consoling. She smiles at her husband. I can't help thinking that it is the kind of beautiful, wholesome, comforting smile that will see him through his worst days. It is a smile I have seen before, on the lips of patients who somehow drag themselves out of their existential suffering to think of others. Although we set up another appointment, she says goodbye, articulating what we both suspect. 'If I don't see you again, thank you for being part of my life. You did your best. You guys have a tough job'.

Her grace leaves me speechless. She dies in the week leading up to Christmas. Her husband calls to say that she went peacefully, even willingly.

On days like this, the word happiness loses its meaning for me. Everything appears hollow. Uncouth, unfair, and unacceptable in the face of the loss of a young woman whose time had not yet come. I mourn for the little girl who lost her mother far too early but feel guilty when I am unable to imagine what that must be like.

Also, I feel the pangs of loss even momentarily imagining being afflicted by an illness that might pull me away from my own children. On these days, happiness is a mirage. I can't fathom how it can be so ephemeral and possibly refuse to land in the lap of a devoted young mother. The consideration of happiness then leads to the perennial question of who deserves to be happy. If we make our own happiness, then what did my young patient do to 'unmake' hers? In all the time I knew her she continued to make room for the happiness of others while watching her own being tugged away. On days like this, I feel satisfied defining happiness as merely avoiding the patient's fate. To expect anything else would be utterly selfish.

On other days, thankfully, these searing moments recede when I see genuinely uplifting things. A patient whom no-one expected to outlive ten months returns for a ten year check up, his once-tender-aged children now grown up, driving him to appointments, and solicitously asking questions about their dad's health. 'They spoil me', he beams.

One woman wrenched from the throes of psychotic depression, convinced that the spectre of breast cancer would forever haunt her life one day holds a healthy baby in her arms. Cradling him as she undresses for an examination, I watch his innocent and placid face entirely unaware of his mother's battle.

'He is adorable', I say, handing him back. With a spark in her eyes where before there was only the dullness of tears, she says, 'Doctor, I never ever think of my cancer any more. It's wonderful, how he takes up all my attention!'

On days like this, I see happiness everywhere. The smiles of my patients, their relieved sighs, their stammered thanks and tentative hugs are the very essence of happiness. These experiences also empower me to help my other patients across the chasm of doubt and pessimism that infects their lives as they confront their own illness. They say: 'I need you to see the bright side for me because I can't yet. But I feel reassured to hear you say that I'll be okay'. Happiness then is being someone's crutch when they are at their most vulnerable. It feels good to give.

A few times a year, I am humbled by an invitation to attend a patient's funeral. Usually, they were people who carried their illness for a long enough time that we came to know each other beyond the confines of a clinical consultation. The sight of my children's wobbly artwork adorning the walls proved a natural and welcome bridge to discussing the things that mattered most in life. Many people told me that despite feeling overwhelmed and frightened by cancer they made sense of it by realising every precious moment with their loved ones. They proposed, married, reconciled, attended graduations, held their grandchild's finger, surfed, walked, wrote letters and generally did all the things they had always known they should do. 'Knowing I am dying makes everything look brand new', a man reflected.

The last funeral I attended was of a dear octogenarian who had insisted on knitting clothes for my three children and always came to see me with an impeccable-looking cake she had baked the night before. On her last visit to hospital, she was so weak that she didn't even notice me until I came very close. Then, recognition flooded her gaunt face and lit it up. She hugged me tightly and told me how pleased she was to see me. I held her gnarled hand and told her that I would look after her. I reassured her that she wouldn't experience pain. That night she died, declaring that after ten years of having cancer and then losing her husband, she had had enough.

I felt a stab of sadness at the finality of her coffin but then, listening to the accounts of her unacceptable decline I felt happy that she was no longer suffering. I felt happy that I had managed to keep her well for so long. I felt happy that she had trimmed her garden and adjusted her furniture in the weeks before dying. And I felt immeasurably relieved and happy that I had accidentally found her in the emergency room, for as it turned out, it was to be our only meeting before she died that night.

The hospital is a revolving door for many of my patients. The chance discovery that a patient has died somewhere in this labyrinthine place without seeing a familiar doctor is distressing. The observation that even when an illness is incurable, there can be comfort from a human touch and a kind presence makes me happy. And sometimes, my feelings of gratitude, humbleness and complete awe mingle into happiness as I realise how privileged I am to be a doctor and be let into the most intimate spaces of people's lives.

These notions of happiness, derived from my professional work, inform my personal life. I don't think happiness is elusive. It is also not as esoteric as people make it out to be. For a start, happiness is the absence of illness and disability and the presence of good health. Not all ill people are unhappy but wellness should surely convey an advantage to happiness. When I watch the small and big ways in which the incapacities of my patients become a thorn in their lives, I am grateful, and hence happy, to have my health intact. Walking along a track lit by the first rays of the sun, hearing the melody of invisible birds, beholding a dewdrop poised ever so keenly on the edge of a leaf – I know all too well that these spontaneous pleasures of my life are far from universal. Many people must plan ahead and summon the required energy to experience them. 'I would happily exchange a shorter life for the joy of walking again', reflected a bed-bound patient.

A very large part of my happiness is derived through my children. My pregnancies were difficult and my first pregnancy ended in the loss of twins. Even my obstetrician thought that

I wouldn't dare try again but such was the pull of motherhood that I went back three times. My children are the pure, unadulterated joy and the proudest feature of my life. They complete a life that I had actually never deemed incomplete before they came along. Their innocence is as endearing as it is moving. Their happiness is infectious because it is delightfully uncomplicated. A scooter ride on the beach with the wind carrying their squeals, 'You are the best mama in the world!' Their suspicion and curiosity when they ask whether I buy the toys on Santa's behalf, forgotten in the next instant as their eyes sparkle at the countdown to his arrival. The thrill of the tooth fairy's visit; the exhilaration of their first plane trip; their incredulity at having their own television screen on a flight! They are not just the stuff of their happiness but very much mine too!

Walking hand in hand to school with a surprise stop at the bakery, redolent with the smell of fresh bread. Helping out in the schoolroom, losing the parent-teacher relay race to the hoarse cheers of the class, watching fireworks dazzle the night sky, reading together. I can't help thinking that precious memories seems to cascade into your life when you have children. And I greedily grab them all. No doubt informed by the patients whose lives are tragically cut short, I have never been one to wait for happiness to come to me. I see happiness in all kinds of incidental and everyday occasions and I don't care if it's unfashionable but I embrace it.

I had an itinerant childhood, growing up and being schooled in many countries. Hand in hand with this wonderful experience came the fact that I constantly had to leave old friends and make new ones. I learned resilience and also that you don't always need other people to make you happy. The laughter and love of family and friends are obviously important but no less vital is the capacity to be content in one's own company. A lot of my work involves the dictum that a sorrow shared is a sorrow halved. I listen to stories of patients who feel unfairly served by life. So at day's end, the only recipe for my happiness can be a quiet space that allows me to read, write and reflect on the responsibility of being a doctor and the privilege of being a mother.

Many of my patients are terminally ill. I see some who chase happiness and end up dissatisfied. Sometimes I can't help thinking that it wouldn't be so elusive if they stopped and looked. But I also meet those who let happiness come to them through simple acts – by adjusting their expectations, reconciling to fate but not being held hostage by it. They don't treat happiness as an external entity, to be had and lost. Instead, happiness filters through their life on a daily basis, discovered in small things. Their grandchild's graduation, the birth of a niece, a fishing trip with their son, a family holiday squeezed in between rounds of chemotherapy. Their happiness comes from enjoying moments that they feared they might not see. These are the people who die contented; they also leave their family consoled and uplifted by their memory.

One should always be judicious with dispensing advice but if I were to give my children a piece of advice on being happy, this is what I think I would say: Work hard at finding a job that feels like a vocation. Look beyond narrow self-interest and tend to the needs of others. Cultivate a still, reflective mind. Have few friends but hold them close. Nurture your family and hold them closer. Regard life as a gift and death as inevitable. While it's impossible to do good and be good every single day, live each day mindfully so that you may learn from your mistakes. I'd like to think that in living by some simple rules, you don't constantly have to beckon happiness. Happiness will come to you.

THE THINGS YOU SHOULDN'T SAY TO AN ABORIGINAL PERSON

Larissa Behrendt

I recently spent some time on an outstation in the Northern Territory. Unless you have been on one, it is hard to understand the level of poverty in which some Aboriginal people live – sleeping on concrete floors, with little money, no luxuries. Life is supplemented with bush tucker and everyone works together and shares what they have. Amongst the basics of life, there is resilience. But there is also something else that is perhaps even more surprising. As I sat around the campfire in the evening, what rose up into the night sky mingled with the smoke was laughter.

This is a community surrounded by tragedy and hard social problems. This is a community where there are deep concerns about the impact of mining on sacred sites, concerns about the access to education, feelings of being disenfranchised and the stresses of having very little money to survive on. In nearby towns, there are issues of substance abuse and violence. So it is easy to fall into cliché and to see this laughter as being cathartic, an important release.

But there is something deeper than just the fleeting laughter that comes at the end of a funny story, a witty comment or a parody. It always strikes me in a close-knit community that there is something much more profound at work. Around a campfire with shared resources – from food, clothes, blankets, to utensils, even shoes – there is a deep sense of contentment, a profound happiness.

A world away from an outstation, I recently sat around for a meal with another group of Aboriginal people. In a lovely Greek restaurant, a circle of young Aboriginal professionals shared our stories about 'things you shouldn't say to an Aboriginal person'. Mine was: 'don't worry, you can't tell'. We were roaring with laughter at the ignorant barbs that had been thrown our way, and amongst each other these things that had been hurtful and humiliating when said by ignorant people were now a source of communal laughter and a bond of shared experience.

My dad grew up in an orphanage before becoming a street kid, and would always tell funny stories about his various antics and pranks. He would always choose to share an entertaining anecdote over telling you about his past hardships. It was only in the final year of his life that he revealed to me that he had suffered from physical and emotional abuse while living there. My father was an extraordinary man. From being forced to leave school at fourteen he ended his professional life teaching at a university as a leading expert on Aboriginal culture and history. Inspired by his own experiences of growing up away from his family, he was one of the founders of the organisation Link-Up that reconnects Aboriginal and Torres Strait Islander people removed from their families. Although my father's early life left him with his own emotional scars, he was never a person who would use that past as an excuse. Instead, he would always find the funny moment and I suspect that this attitude to life enabled him to eventually come to terms with the demons in his past, and live the last part of his life in a happiness that he deserved.

This experience of looking at the funny side through adversity is not unique, and it certainly seems to be an important survival mechanism. Sean Choolburra has worked as a stand-up comedian for just over a decade, and is now the best known Aboriginal comedian. His parents grew up on Palm Island – a place where curfews were imposed, and where segregation thrived. A leprosy colony was built on the next island. 'But you wouldn't know it was tragic or horrific', he says, 'my mum, dad and grandparents would tell all these funny yarns over tea and dampers. Hearing all these, you would have thought they had the greatest lives growing up. But you got the sense that they wouldn't have survived without our sense of humour'.

'The flip side of tragedy is comedy', says Aboriginal stand-up comedian Kevin Kropinyeri. 'We have had to learn to look at our situation. We never had much on the mission without. My nana would spend three month periods in gaol for being off the mission without papers. Laughter is healing and is a way of coping with life'.

The 1986 short film *Babakiueria* was based on a concept of Aboriginal people discovering white people and their sacred places (for example 'the barbecue area'). A white family struggles to cope with the assault on their way of life as their world is taken over by Aboriginal people. It remains one of the most cutting satirical looks at the hypocrisy of white perspectives on Aboriginal people, culture and history – not just a humorous comedy sketch, but a film that provokes people to think about their prejudices.

Basically Black, which aired on the ABC in 1973, had an ensemble cast that included Gary Foley and Bob Mazza, who did sketch comedy. It explored 'reverse racism' and included a character called Super Boong. It was ripe with parody of the double standards by which Aboriginal people were forced to live, and was confrontational about the overt racism that was still so prevalent in Australian society at that time. The cleverness of *Basically Black* was that it seduced its audience with humour – it delivered a powerful punch that engaged an audience who would not have tuned in if the tone were one of preachy self-righteousness. It managed to engage them in a conversation with Aboriginal people in a way they might not have otherwise.

It's hard to imagine such audacious and raw satire on the television screens at the moment. The coverage of Indigenous issues has become very serious and, while that is an appropriate way to deal with the serious issues that still face Aboriginal and Torres Strait Islander communities around the country, we seem to have lost something when we lost our sense of humour.

But happiness isn't just laughter. Happiness is a broader concept.

I wonder what can be learnt about happiness from the Aboriginal women on the outstation that can illuminate the world for the rest of us. They look at the world around them and they see its riches. They look at the sky and understand its meanings. They look to the land and sea around them and see additional sources of food. They look at the people who make up their family and community, and they see the blessings in what they have. They tell stories of their fishing and hunting trips, of great romances and funny anecdotes. Their world is full of rich stories, of song lines, of music, of dance. Amongst this, it is impossible not to be struck by the deep interconnectedness that they have with each other and with the world around them.

When you have so very little, you are reliant on the people around you. You rely on them to share resources, to help you get from one place to another, to join together to confront a school that is not working with the community or a land council that has not been negotiating properly. And through this meaningful reliance on each other – where you don't just take, but give what you have – there is a deep human connection.

This interconnectedness with other people is essential for a sense of self and a sense of self-worth – a grounding in one's own identity, one's own value, one's own place in the world. And there is also interconnectedness to the natural world. The women on the outstation have been hunting turtles and fishing in the waters since they were small girls. They know which plants are edible and they know what fruit is edible. They know the stories about the creation of the world around them, how the constellations in the sky were formed, and the songlines about great trips across the country. In the world around them, there are stories and legends, and a knowledge of the seasons and an ability to read the landscape and the weather.

There is something else that engages the women on the outstation that is linked to their culture but also seems to be a basic element in fundamental happiness. They have a very rich creative life. The women of this community – and some of the men – are gifted painters. They translate the stories told by their parents and grandparents into vivid canvasses. They express themselves as eloquently through their brush strokes as they do with their words. And between the painting, the dancing and the music is a rich tradition of storytelling that is as old as the culture. These women are natural storytellers.

They are the expression of the vibrancy of the world's oldest living culture.

These are women who, although amongst the poorest in socio-economic terms, are about the richest in culture, community and creative expression. They value their relationships with other people. They are resourceful. And they find the beauty – and humour – in the simplest things in life. And there is something in the heart of these traditional values that gives rise to foundations for a deep contentment that comes from being grounded in one's self and situation.

There is one other element in the contented happiness that I find in the world of the outstation.

Living in close proximity to others isn't easy, and this is a community where there is overcrowding. On fine nights, people sleep under the stars. But there aren't enough rooms for the number of people here and so people share concrete floors when they have to. So life is not without its arguments and disagreements, its jealousies and bickering, and all of the other things that happen between people who live closely. But the generosity and openness of the women who have the moral leadership in this community is defined by the love they have for their families, especially their children. This is a very real part of the way of life here – happiness is love.

I recently finished a three-year study with colleagues of mine looking at six Aboriginal communities in NSW. Three had high crime rates and three had low crime rates. The purpose of the study was to try to identify the dynamics that separated the communities that thrive from the ones that are dysfunctional. The study was complex and the findings complicated, but one key factor that emerged from the research was that communities that do well often have a group of people within them – mostly women – who assert a kind of moral authority over other people. When they speak or act, others respect them, listen and pitch in. It allows them, as a community, to address issues such as substance abuse and school attendance. In the communities with high crime rates, this moral authority has been eroded long ago. While there are wise, hard-working and reliable people in the community, they do not get the respect or are not able to lead cultural change, especially amongst the younger members of the community.

This finding was not surprising though it was interesting to see it articulated so clearly. The finding is consistent with what I have observed in other parts of Australia, including the Northern Territory. The communities that have the most entrenched social problems are the ones where the moral authority of the Elders has been undermined long ago, and with this unravelling of the social fabric, there is little ability to lead by example, or be an agent of change within the community. But in the communities that are healthy, there is leadership. These are the communities which find solutions to their problems when they arrive. They are usually communities, like the outstation I visit, which are dry by choice. They are the ones who have developed community buses, programs for children, who look after the elderly and have devised a number of practical solutions to the problems they face. With this ability, which is self-determination in action, comes a strong sense that community members have the capacity to deal with the issues that life throws at them. It is a stark contrast to the communities where social problems are so tenacious and rife that most feel they are powerless to make changes to improve life for the better.

There is no romance in being poor, but there is happiness to be found when you can find the richness in life. This is the abiding lesson I learn from my visits to this other way of life.

And as the laughter rings around the campfire, and I listen to the women, all sisters, sing their songs, teach the children to dance, tell their ancient stories, gently tease each other – and me – I am reminded that there are ties that are deeper than blood and that lightness of spirit is the measure of happiness.

CONTRIBUTORS

James Arvanitakis is the Head of the Academy at the University of Western Sydney, a member of the Institute for Culture and Society, and is a Visiting Research Associate, School of Social Sciences, University of the Witwatersrand. His research interests include citizenship, piracy and innovative teaching pedagogies. His publications include *Piracy: Leakages from Modernity* (2014) and *Contemporary Society: A Sociological Analysis of Everyday Life* (2009). In 2012 he received the Prime Minister's University Teacher of the Year Award.

Brock Bastian is Australian Research Council Future Fellow in the School of Psychology at the University of New South Wales. His research is in the areas of moral reasoning, moral vitalism, dehumanisation and the social norms for happiness. He has published extensively in journals such as the *Psychological Bulletin* and the *Journal of Personality and Social Psychology*.

Larissa Behrendt is a Eualeyai/Kamillaroi woman. She is Professor of Law and Director of the Jumbunna Indigenous House of Learning at the University of Technology, Sydney. Her research focuses on legal and Indigenous social justice issues and her books include *Indigenous Australia for Dummies* (2012),

Aboriginal Dispute Resolution (1995) and *Achieving Social Justice* (2003). She has also published two novels.

Jenny Cameron is Associate Professor in Geography and Environmental Studies at the University of Newcastle, Australia. Her research is in the areas of community and diverse economies. She is co-author of *Take Back the Economy: An Ethical Guide for Transforming our Communities* (with J. K. Gibson-Graham and Stephen Healy, 2013).

Steven Connor is Grace 2 Professor of English at the University of Cambridge and researches in a wide range of areas including cultural phenomenology, sound, atmosphere, art and architecture. His books include *Paraphernalia: The Curious Lives of Magical Things* (2011), *Beyond Words: Sobs, Hums, Stutters and Other Vocalizations* (2014) and *Beckett, Modernism and the Material Imagination* (2014).

J. K. Gibson-Graham is the pen name of the late Julie Graham, and Katherine Gibson who is Professor at the Institute for Culture and Society at the University of Western Sydney. Gibson-Graham's research focuses on rethinking economies as sites of ethical action and her recent publications include *Take Back the Economy: An Ethical Guide for Transforming our Communities* (with Jenny Cameron and Stephen Healy, 2013), *A Postcapitalist Politics* (2006) and *The End of Capitalism (As We Knew It): A Feminist Critique of Political Economy* (1996).

Clive Hamilton is Professor of Public Ethics at Charles Sturt University. He is well known in Australia as a public intellectual and for his contributions to public policy debate, and for founding the think tank, the Australia Institute. His interests encompass the philosophical and ethical dimensions of climate change and economics and his publications include *Earthmasters: The Dawn of the Age of Climate Engineering*, *Silencing Dissent* (edited with Sarah Maddison, 2007) and *Affluenza* (with Richard Denniss, 2005). He is also a member of the Climate Change Authority.

Richard Hamilton is a Lecturer in Philosophy at the University of Notre Dame Australia, Fremantle campus. He specialises in moral philosophy with a particular interest in virtue ethics and the philosophy of biology. He has published in journals such as *Theory, Culture and Society* and the *Journal for the Theory of Social Behaviour*.

Stephen Healy is a Senior Research Fellow at the Institute for Culture and Society at the University of Western Sydney. His researches interests include community economies, Marxist theory, subjectivity, psychoanalytic theory. He is co-author of *Take Back the Economy: An Ethical Guide for Transforming our Communities* (with J. K. Gibson and Jenny Cameron, 2013).

Anna Kamaralli lectures in drama and Shakespeare studies. She has published in journals such as *Shakespeare Survey* and *Shakespeare Bulletin*, on topics ranging from the representation of women on stage, to the depiction of rehearsal in film, to innovative methods for teaching Shakespeare. She is author of *Shakespeare and the Shrew: Performing the Defiant Female Voice* (2012).

Georgina Ledvinka is a Lecturer in English Literature at the University of Notre Dame Australia, Sydney campus. She was previously a practising lawyer and Senior Lecturer in Law in the UK, specialising in socially just legal practice and clinical legal education. Her research interests include representations of gender and religion in children's fiction and she has published in journals including *International Research in Children's Literature*.

Tony Moore is a Senior Lecturer in Communications and Media Studies at Monash University, where he was Director of the National Centre for Australian Studies 2010–13. His research areas include Australian history, media, popular culture, artistic bohemia and politics in the scholarly publications and in the press, radio and television. His books include *Dancing With Empty Pockets: Australia's Bohemians Since 1860* (2012) and *Death or Liberty: Rebels and Radicals Transported to Australia, 1788–1868* (2010). Tony has enjoyed careers as a documentary maker at the ABC and as a publisher.

Camilla Nelson is a Senior Lecturer in Writing at the University of Notre Dame Australia, Sydney campus. She publishes in the fields of creativity, cultural history and popular culture. Her publications include the novels *Perverse Acts* (1999) and *Crooked* (2009) and a wide range of scholarly and journalistic essays.

Deborah Pike is a Senior Lecturer in English Literature at the University of Notre Dame Australia, Sydney campus, and has published in the areas of cultural studies, postcolonial, and modernist literatures. She previously held posts at the University of Paris VII, Denis-Diderot and Paris Institute of Political Studies (Sciences Po). She is co-editor of *Multidisciplinary Perspectives on Play from Early Childhood and Beyond* (with Sandra Lynch and Cynthia a'Beckett, forthcoming 2015).

Alice Pung is a writer, lawyer and teacher. She is currently Artist in Residence at Janet Clarke Hall, the University of Melbourne. Her books include *Laurinda* (2014), *Her Father's Daughter* (2011) and *Unpolished Gem* (2006), and she is editor of *Growing Up Asian in Australia* (2008), an anthology of stories from Asian Australians.

John Quiggin is Professor of Economics at the University of Queensland. He is author of many publications including *Zombie Economics: How Dead Ideas Still Walk Among Us* (2010) as well as *Great Expectations: Microeconomic Reform in Australia* (1996). He is also a member of the Climate Change Authority.

David Ritter is the Chief Executive Officer of Greenpeace Australia Pacific, an Honorary Fellow at the School of Law at the University of Western Australia and an Associate of the Sydney Democracy Network of the University of Sydney. He has extensive experience in campaigning for environmental and social justice issues as well as research and writing in the areas of legal history and native title. He is author of *The Native Title Market* (2009) and *Contesting Native Title* (2009).

Ranjana Srivastava is an oncologist and a Fulbright scholar in the Australian public health system who writes on health-related matters. Her books include *So It's Cancer, Now What?* (2014); *Dying for a Chat: The Communication Breakdown Between Doctors and Patients* (2012), the winner of the Human Rights Literature Prize; and *Tell Me the Truth: Conversations with my Patients about Life and Death* (2010), shortlisted for the NSW Premier's Literary Prize. Her columns appear regularly in the *Guardian* and Fairfax Media and she has appeared widely on television and radio.